PRAISE FOR CONRAD SCHMIDT'S
Alternatives to Growth: Efficiency Shifting

Alternatives to Grov... ...ook I have
read on climate ch... the
interconnectednes
Revolution, the eco... _ social and
cultural interdepenc... ...our human
communities – all in 150 pages! He describes the false hope
and environmental and social devastation that unlimited
growth and a consumption based lifestyle has produced.
Conrad presents solutions to the combined crises of climate
change, energy stress, poverty and wealth inequity, and
environmental degradation. It's one thing to understand how
we got to a place where radical and rapid change is
necessary, it's another to provide the blueprint for how that
change can happen so that it feels simple and straightforward
and safe. That's exactly what *efficiency shifting* does and the
solutions are powerful on many levels. Most important for
me is understanding that we'll not just create lots of new jobs
as we transform to a sustainable economy, we'll recreate
meaningful work. Conrad's prescriptions serve the dual
function of improving our communities and the environment
<u>and</u> letting people know that their labour and intellect are of
value to the greater good.

- Jane Sterk, leader of the Green Party of BC

Conrad Schmidt hits the ecological nail on the head once again with "Efficiency Shifting." As with Workers of the World Relax, Schmidt understands that humanity cannot grow itself out of its dilemma of overshoot. Growth is our problem. In this book he describes the only path that will help us restore a genuinely sustainable society. We cannot just continue to create meaningless work, but must rediscover fundamental values of nature, family, community, and the time-honoured practice of just hanging out with each other.

*- Rex Weyler, author, Greenpeace: The Inside Story.
Co-founder of Greenpeace International.*

With his new book, EFFICIENCY SHIFTING, Conrad Schmidt shows once again what a truly creative and out-of-the-box thinker he is. This excellent primer provides a whole new paradigm for thinking about the economy. It offers real potential of pulling us away from our present chaotic and unsustainable economic course and finding our future jobs among the caring and earth-friendly activities that are not "profitable" in our current market-driven world. EFFICIENCY SHIFTING deserves a wide readership!

- John de Graaf. Director, Take Back Your Time and co-author, Affluenza: The all-consuming epidemic

Conrad's refreshing take on the need for heavy investment in the labour intensive sectors of a healthy and caring society, makes ecological and financial sense. It's a quick read and thoughtful reframe on how to create a softer landing for carbon overdosed economies.

- Joel Solomon. Renewal Partners

Conrad@ragTAGproductions.net

604- 346 - 1328

Alternatives to Growth

Alternatives to Growth:

Efficiency Shifting

By Conrad Schmidt

Published 2009

ISBN 978-0-9739772-2-6

Printed and Bound in Canada

For Mika

Who inspired me to write this book

ACKNOWLEDGEMENTS

It is impossible to give enough thanks to all the people who have contributed to this book. This book has truly been a collaborative effort. Many of the ideas are the culmination of fun coffee shop discussions and bottles of red wine with good friends.

I am indebted to Stoo Abraham who rescued the first part of the book and to my good friend Dave Herbert who's colourful writing style added to its charm. Dave Herbert also provided much of the book's direction. The background and historical context came after many years of discussions with my friend and fellow Luddite Tom Walker. A special thanks goes to Sasha Schmidt, Andrea Curtis, Chris Nolan, Julian Oettle, Jessica Paul-Masson, Arne Hansen, Garth Mullins, Diane Macdonald, Kevin Stiller, Irene Stupka, Gudren Langolf, Bill Tubs, Ivan Doumenc, Greg Hamilton, David Maidman, Ian Gregson, Matt Hern and Walter Ross for their support, feedback and ideas.

The editing was done by Michelle Vergeer, Stoo Abraham, Paul Halychuk and my life partner Chantal Morin. The illustrations were done by Andrea Curtis.

Writing this book with all your help and guidance has been a lot of fun. Thank you.

It seems that the ecologically necessary is politically unfeasible, but the politically feasible is ecologically irrelevant.

William Rees, Professor, University of British Columbia

CONTENTS

INTRODUCTION

It seems we have an annoying problem. Infinite growth on a finite planet is logistically impossible. There is a hard wired limit telling us that we can't consume, build and pollute indefinitely. More than annoying, over the last two decades it has become a reality: 60 percent of the world's ecosystems are in decline.[1] The effects of climate change have become increasingly visible and difficult to deny. Of course we can do what we have been doing for the last 40 years and simply ignore it. A simple solution that, so far, seems just as effective as anything else being proposed by our world leaders. But it is not the only solution.

Most of the debate on what to do about the ecological crisis has been centred around two perspectives:

- Green Growth: More efficient toasters, cars and buildings. A new generation of green consumers that will rescue the economy and the ecology. Or as the slogan goes, "buying a sustainable planet."

- No Growth: If it is impossible to grow the economy indefinitely, how about we just don't do that? With more equitable distribution we can all afford to slow down the wheels of industry, consume less and have a much better standard of living, which is a good argument and one that I have been a proponent of for many years. Up until a few months ago, I was a firm believer that the engines of growth simply had to stop. This is still my preferred solution, but I now concede that there is a third option.

Efficiency Shifting

Even though it is impossible to grow the economy indefinitely, not all the economy needs to grow. We have the option of balancing efficiencies in some sectors with increasing inefficiencies in others. The idea that I put forward is that some sectors, in particular the social and caring sectors, would benefit from actually becoming inefficient. This theory is different from the theory of steady state economy because it's about creating a dynamic equilibrium within the economy that still allows many of the benefits of growth with no net overall industrial growth. More than that, it also makes it possible to shrink the overall economy with very few negative side effects.

For many years I believed that there was no option other than simply switching off the engines of growth. The concept of efficiency shifting has changed my mind. It is also an option that will satisfy more than simple Luddites like myself.

Note:

1. Millennium Ecosystem Assessment, 2005, The Millennium Ecosystem Assessment (MA) was drawn up by 1,300 researchers from 95 nations over four years.

PART 1
Legacy of the Industrial Revolution

Chapter 1
Something Important the Media Forgot to Mention

In 2007, the American economy went into recession. By 2009, many of the world's economies had followed suit. Prior to the recession, several surveys had shown that the environment was either the number one concern for citizens or a growing concern.[1] After the recession hit, the number one concern became the economy. Jobs were lost, homes repossessed and hardly a word was heard on the relationship between the economy and ecology. There were even a few newspaper articles about how a reduction in funding to environmental groups was going to put more of the ecology in jeopardy. Amidst all the fear about the economy, a lot of good news got lost.

The good news that went largely unreported was that this recession gave parts of the environment a bit of a breather. Decades of unending growth had taken a toll on the ecology. A shrinking economy was giving the ecology time to repair.

Decreased housing construction in the US has resulted in a corresponding decrease in logging in Canada's ancient Great Bear Rainforest. Elk and wolf populations are on the rise. In urban areas the use of car co-ops, carpooling, public transit and cycling is increasing.

More good news for the environment followed when General Motors filed for bankruptcy in 2009. In the United Kingdom, car production was down 55 percent. During the first four months of 2009, 293,000 fewer cars were manufactured in the UK. [2] General Motors alone produced 650,586 fewer cars from January to June 2009 than in the same period in 2008. From an ecological perspective this is significant. An average car contains over 3,200 pounds of steel, iron, plastics, aluminium, glass, rubber, fluids, lubricants, lead, zinc, platinum, copper and other materials. By the time it leaves the assembly line it has generated 29 tons of solid waste and 1,207 million cubic yards of air pollution.[3]

International Air Transport Association traffic data showed air travel demand had fallen for the ninth straight month, down more than nine percent in May 2009.[4] The ecological benefit was again significant. Commercial aviation is responsible for about three percent of global carbon emissions.[5] A single return transatlantic flight between London and New York produces about 1.2 tons of CO2 emissions[6] per passenger, the equivalent of driving a car for about six months. This global decline in air travel continued from 2008, when several airlines filed for bankruptcy (Zoom, ATA Airlines, Skybus Airlines and Aloha). Rather than fly nearly empty planes, airlines were cancelling flights and grounding planes. Many orders for new planes were cancelled. For the year 2009 Boeing had 85 orders for its new Dreamliner 787, and 84 cancellations. That is a total of one order for 2009.[7] The new Airbus A380 is also seeing similar cancellations.

There was more good news for the environment. In Singapore, idling ships clogged the shoreline. How is that good news? First some background. Singapore is the world's busiest port. Normally ships arrive, unload and load within an average of 10 days. Global trade was down, however, and fewer ships were crossing the oceans. Many of these ships had no onward destination and just stayed, clogging the waters. This is good news because shipping is one of the biggest polluters. Confidential data from maritime industry insiders shows that based on engine size and fuel type, just 15 of the world's biggest ships may now emit as much pollution as all the world's 760 million cars. Low-grade ship bunker fuel (or fuel oil) has up to 2,000 times the sulphur content of the diesel fuel used in US and European automobiles. Every ship that remains in port is an ecological lifeline.[8]

With fewer cars, planes and other items being manufactured, there is a corresponding decline in the price of raw materials. The price of copper, aluminium and other commodities fell approximately 40 percent by June 2009. This might not be what shareholders of mining corporations want to hear, but for the ecology few things could be better. Mining, particularly open pit mining, has an enormous ecological impact. According to the US Environmental Protection Agency, mining activities in the United States (not counting coal) produce between one and two billion tons of mine waste annually. These mines (not including coal) are responsible for polluting over 3,400 miles of streams and 440,000 acres of land. [9]

We can examine the basic relationship between mining and manufacturing and how a decrease in manufacturing is helpful. Copper mining, for example, will produce on average 99 tons of waste rock per ton of copper. A single Boeing 747, one of the most popular jets ever produced, requires approximately five tons of copper to manufacture it. So every 747 order cancelled means 500 tons of rock does not need to be mined, processed, and disposed. This also means a decreased release of hazardous chemicals such as heavy metals, acid-producing sulfides, and other contaminates into surrounding ecosystems.

A long and disconcerting aspect of mining is that it often displaces indigenous people who reside where mining companies want to operate. In addition mining operations poison the air, soil, and water on which the indigenous people depend. In January 2007 hundreds of police, army and corporate security personnel descended on the small rural communities of the indigenous Q'eqchi' in Guatemala. Their homes were torched and their belongings destroyed. They were forced to leave the land. The reason was that a Canadian mining firm called Sky Resource Mining was opening up a nickel mine. Nickel mining, like most mining, is highly toxic to the local ecology. It destroys local wildlife and pollutes local water tables. The Q'eqchi' have lived, hunted and farmed on the land for hundreds of years. One of the things pushing up the price of nickel was demand for batteries in such things as Hybrid cars. In 2008 the price of nickel collapsed and consequently the mine was never built. And in 2009 the Q'eqchi' were able to return to their homes. Another quasi-victory for the ecology and this time for people as well. [10]

By decreasing air travel, airplane production, demand for copper and other mined materials, we can hopefully decrease the effects of mining on both the environment and indigenous people.

A particular piece of good news: one of the world's worst ongoing environmental disasters faces a downturn thanks to the temporary falling price of oil. The Alberta Oil Sands contain the majority of known oil deposits in North America, but they are also the most polluting. The Canadian oil sands will produce more CO_2 emissions than the rest of the Canadian economy. Production of a barrel of tar sands oil generates three times more carbon emissions than a barrel of normal crude.[11] The oil sands is a massive project, causing the displacement of enough earth to fill the Toronto's Skydome or New York's Yankee Stadium every single day. One company alone, Syncrude, emitted the equivalent greenhouse gases of 2.7 million cars in 2005 (a staggering 10.3 million tonnes). As a result of lower oil prices, some new projects in the Tar Sands have stopped. On July 22 2009, Suncor Energy, the biggest Canadian oil-sands producer, posted its third straight quarterly loss after crude prices plunged.[12] In addition, a large Trailbreaker pipeline that would have delivered oil to US refineries has been temporarily shelved. [13]

According to the Organization of Petroleum Exporting Countries (OPEC), the demand for oil has fallen by about 1.56 million barrels per day as a result of the economic slowdown.[14] The increase in the world's emissions from fossil fuel burning and cement production in 2008 halved.[15] The downturn is doing what climate change deals such as the Kyoto protocol have never been able to succeed at. These figures do not even account for all the other pollution, such as mercury and sulfur, from which the ecology is being spared.

A slowed down economy is succeeding where our human goodwill has completely failed. When it comes to a decision between profit and the environment, governments have always chosen profit. However, the slower economy is reducing the profit motive.

According to Alex Bowen, an economist with the Grantham Research Institute on Climate Change and the Environment at the London School of Economics, the rule of thumb used is that a 1 percent change in GDP brings a 0.9 percent change in carbon pollution. This means the 2.5 percent decline in worldwide GDP for 2009 projected by the International Monetary Fund, would reduce emissions by 2.25 percent. [15]

In Ireland for example, experts say the recession has cut GDP by nine percent, taking it back to 2005 levels. This has probably reduced annual greenhouse gas emissions by the same amount, within the limits permitted under Kyoto. [16]

The benefits of a contracting overall economy for the ecology are clear. A shrinking economy has, so far, been the only thing that has any credibility in reducing our ecological footprint. The economic slowdown is succeeding where all protocols and eco-favourable legislation have failed.

However, a shrinking economy, even though it is good for the ecology and for many indigenous people, does not have popular appeal for the majority of the population. For many, it represents jobs lost, homes repossessed, depression and anxiety. It is easy to say that we need to shrink the economy to achieve ecological balance, but if it results in large masses of unemployed people, it is unlikely to get the needed support.

The solution required is one that correctly recognizes the balance between the ecology, society and the economy. Unlimited industrial growth is not a solution for the ecology or the economy, but unemployment and poverty are not options that people will willingly accept.

The solution of efficiency shifting is an attempt to balance these conflicting goals by not stagnating the overall economy, but creating a dynamic balance between efficiency and inefficiency within the economy that will achieve some of the desired social needs and benefits from growth.

When we look at historical charts of carbon emission in the atmosphere, they are fairly stable for the majority of human history on the planet. They only start to rise from the beginning of the Industrial Revolution. This is where our analysis begins.

Notes:

1. Canwest News Service. July 28, 2009. Financial Post: *Economy edges out terrorism, environment as Canadians' top concern: survey.* Retrieved from: http://www.financialpost.com

2. BBC News Services. 22 May, 2009. *Car production down 55% in April.* Retrieved from: http://news.bbc.co.uk

3. Alvord, Katie T. 2000. New Society Publishers. *Divorce Your Car!: Ending the Love Affair with the Automobile.* ISBN: 08-86571-408-8. Page 84.

4. Financial Post. June 25, 2009.

5. Philander, George. 2008. SAGE: Los Angeles. *Encyclopedia of Global Warming and Climate Change.* ISBN: 9781412958783. Volume 1: Page 107.

6. Monbiot, George. 2008. Doubleday of Canada. *Heat: How to Stop the Planet Burning.* ISBN-10: 0385662211. Page 173.

7. Reuters. Jul 2, 2009. *Boeing says 17 plane orders cancelled in last week.* Retrieved from: http://www.reuters.com

8. Guardian UK. April 9, 2009. *Health risks of shipping pollution have been 'underestimated'.* Retrieved from: http://www.guardian.co.uk.

BBC News. September 18, 2009. *Aboard the world's biggest cargo ship.* Retrieved from: http://news.bbc.co.uk

9. MSE Technology Applications, Inc. for :US Environmental Protection Agency. *2005 Annual Report: Mine Waste Technology.*

10. Interview with Reverend Emilie Smith, a minister with the Anglican Church in Guatemala. She is currently documenting the experiences of the Q'eqchi people in a book still to be published titled Gold Lust.

11. Nikiforuk, Andrew. 2008. Greystone Books: Vancouver, BC. *Tar Sands: Dirty Oil and the Future of a Continent.* ISBN: 978-1-55365-407-0. Page 119.

12. Laverty, Gene. July 22, 2009. *Suncor Posts Third Quarterly Loss on Lower Oil Prices.* Retrieved from: http://www.bloomberg.com.

13. Bloomberg. January 18, 2009

14. OPEC. World Oil Outlook 2009

15. Duncan Clark. Guardian. Growth of global carbon emissions halved in 2008, say Dutch researchers. June 25 2009

16. David Adam. Guardian UK. Will the recession cut our CO2 emissions? February 23 2009

Chapter 2
The Industrial Revolution

The most famous economic slowdown is the Great Depression of the 1930s. Equally interesting, there was a much smaller recession that happened in England following the invention of the spinning jenny in 1764. The story marks the beginning of the Industrial Revolution, a revolution that has not yet come to an end, and provides a graphic demonstration of how technology changes society.

Prior to the invention of the spinning jenny, yarn (the thread used to make fabric) was spun one spindle at a time, which was a time and labour-intensive process. Spinning yarn and then weaving it into fabric constituted a large part of daily farm life. Days were spent tending livestock and farming, the nights spinning yarn and weaving. The income kept local rural communities functioning. Traditionally, women spun yarn and men weaved it into fabrics. Families worked and stayed together, communities were close knit.

Since every single thread of every item of clothing had to be spun one thread at a time, and then woven into cloth, fabric was very expensive. A single item of clothing could easily represent more than a month of labour. As cloth was so dear, possession of anything more than two sets of clothes was considered conspicuous consumption, a luxury only to be enjoyed by the rich. For most of the population, all that was necessary was one set of clothes to wear and another to be washed. Fashion changed very slowly, nothing like the seasonal fads of today. Dress of the seventeenth century was not all that different from that of the sixteenth or fifteenth century.

The most time-intensive part of the entire fabric making process was spinning yarn. It generally took three yarn spinners to keep one weaver busy. Eager to capitalize on solving this production bottleneck, a group of intrepid businessmen offered a reward of fifty pounds to anyone who could invent a machine capable of spinning six threads at once. Fifty pounds might not sound like a lot in today's inflationary economy, but it is equivalent to about 50,000 pounds today. Many inventors took up the challenge without immediate success. It took three years before the prize was finally claimed by an inventor named James Hargreaves. The invention was named the spinning jenny. It proved to be the technological wonder of its day, a device that would not only revolutionize industry, but would also overthrow everything from social order to family structure.

Four months after the first machine was built, a second machine that could spin twenty threads was unveiled. A year later, a third, that could spin 120 strands of yarn at once, was built. The bottleneck of cloth manufacturing was broken. It was now possible for one yarn spinner to keep seven or eight weavers busy. Yarn spinning and weaving factories started to appear. The first factory in England was another one of Mr. Hargreaves' ideas.[1] The increasingly efficient machines and the inauguration of the factory system represented a transition between two distinct ways of life. For the first time, labourers, generally women and children, began to leave their homes and communities to go and work in factories. This was a blow to the historically sacred family structure and infuriated many. During the beginning of the Industrial

Revolution conditions in the initial factories were harsh. With no laws protecting labourers, twelve hour days and six day work weeks were not uncommon. There were also no minimum wage standards. For those that were unwilling to accept harsh working conditions for very little money, there were the Poor Laws; laws that rather than helped the poor, imposed brutal living conditions on them.

Another unforeseen consequence of the spinning jenny and other similar machines was the collapse of the price of yarn. Far fewer yarn spinners were needed to spin enough yarn to meet market demand. The cost of labour was sharply reduced. As a side effect, seven out of eight yarn spinners - the women who were not willing or able to leave their families to go and work in factories - were thrown out of work. This was not a happy state of affairs for many.

In the case of James Hargreaves, protests quickly arose. Disgruntled yarn spinners (plus their families that depended on the income from home spinning and weaving) rioted. The protesters broke into Mr Hargreaves' factory, smashed his machines, and sent him fleeing to Nottingham for his life.

It took some time, but from this and similar events, a powerful revolutionary movement would grow. In the early nineteenth century, the infamous Luddites, an army of anti-technocrats that yearned for the good old days of cottage industry and community, smashed and burned factories and the machines they housed throughout England. Their numbers and training grew to the point where they were capable of direct military confrontation with the British army. They were seen as such a severe threat to the fabric of society that destroying a machine was declared an offence punishable by death.

What eventually brought civility back to England was not the harsh crackdown by the army, but rather a change in consumer habits. People started to consume more. Wildly radical ideas, such as changing one's underwear weekly arose. The new cotton clothes were not only cheaper, but also more comfortable. Demand for textiles grew and people who were formerly jobless gained new employment.

New jobs were not only found in textiles. Even though the efficiency of machines resulted in a loss of jobs, it also freed up labour to new and growing industries. A surplus in labour translates to an opportunity for people to move into newly emerging industries. The steam age of locomotion, ships and mechanization would not have been possible if the population was at home spinning yarn and slowly weaving fabric in small cottage industries.

The tale of the spinning jenny and the Luddites would weave itself through many threads throughout history. This was just the beginning of a pattern that would repeat more rapidly as industrialization continued:

The more efficient we become, the more we need to consume. Technology makes us more efficient, with less labour we can produce more. If we do not consume more we end up with a surplus of labour and people lose their jobs. However, a surplus in labour is key in further industrial growth. Consumption of new products increases and the economy grows and employment rises.

This journey also marks the beginning of potentially the greatest threat to mankind. For thousands of years prior to the Industrial Revolution and its machines, the level of greenhouse gases was relatively consistent at about 280 parts per million (ppm). By 1950, it had risen to 310 ppm. The concentration of carbon dioxide in the atmosphere as of 2009 stands at 387 parts per million (ppm). This represents an increase of 40 percent since the beginning of the Industrial revolution.[2]

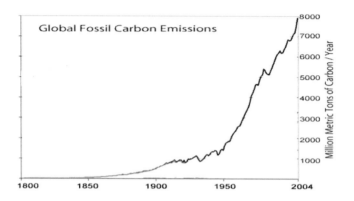

Notes:

1. Thwaite, Benjamin Howarth. 1882. Oxford University: London. *Our factories, workshops, and warehouses: their sanitary and fire-resisting.* Lccn: 07024727. Page 7.

2. Amphal, S. S. R. 1992. Island Press: Washington, DC. *Our country, the planet: forging a partnership for survival.* ISBN: 1-55963-165-1. Page 79.

3. This figure is original and was prepared for Commons by Mak Thorpe using data from available at US Department of Energy web page. Original Data citation: Marland, G., T.A. Boden, and R. J. Andres. 2007. *Global, Regional, and National CO2 Emissions. In Trends: A Compendium of Data on Global Change.* Carbon Dioxide Information Analysis Center, Oak Ridge National Laboratory.

Chapter 3
The Story of Henry Ford and the Great Depression

As the nineteenth century drew to a close and the twentieth century began, there was a wave of new technological inventions that made industry vastly more efficient and able to produce far more goods than ever before. The invention of the combustion engine, the automobile, production/assembly lines, the radio, telegraphy and mechanized farming were all significant, but the biggest single development in producing more goods and services came from the electrification of industry. Factories with assembly lines, driven by electric motors worked around the clock, mass producing goods in unheard of quantities and at unprecedented speed.

Today the idea of continuous mass production seems the norm, but it was not always so. This new level of industrialization was created in 1912 by the Ford Motor Company in Highlands Park, Michigan. Economist Edward A. Filene described this as the beginning of the second Industrial Revolution.[1]

Henry Ford was born in 1863 on the family farm near a rural town west of Detroit, Michigan. His letters from these early years show that he did not much care for farming. His passion was more for tinkering and repairing machines. In his early teens, his father gave him a pocket watch. The watch, rumour has it, was quickly taken apart, studied and then reassembled.

His father, with whom Henry had a fairly tense relationship, wanted him to go into the family business. However, his love of mechanics would lead him in a different direction. In 1879, at the age of 16, he left home to work as an apprentice machinist in Detroit.

In 1891, Ford became an engineer with the Edison Illuminating Company, which specialized in the construction of electrical generating stations. Two short years later he was promoted to chief engineer, a very quick rise to the top. The industry of electricity was still in its infancy and Ford was ideally placed to learn the skills that would set him apart from his competition: knowledge of power generators and electric motors, and the potential they had to offer.

In 1899, Ford quit his job as chief engineer. He had developed a new obsession with the horseless carriage and wanted to devote as much time as possible to finding new ways to improve its design. His passion for gas-powered automobiles eventually culminated in the establishment of the Ford Motor Company in 1901.

In those days, start-up costs were relatively small and excitement in this new technology was high. Consequently there were many manufacturers all competing to gain market share. Initially, Ford's company was not very different from all the others scraping by. Struggling and often on the verge of bankruptcy, the Ford Motor Company managed to produce 1745 automobiles in 1904.

Automobiles of that era were individually crafted, hand-built by teams of highly skilled engineers who were knowledgeable in many aspects of construction. Many cars were tailor-made. Workrooms were cluttered with all the tools required by teams of craftsmen. Large crews and equipment competed for space at different production stations. Manual labour, and occasionally gravity, were the only forms of power available to move all the heavy equipment through the factory.

Henry Ford was well aware of the problems of static construction. To him, it was evident that an assembly line would be the solution. Instead of moving the factory around the automobile, move the automobile. This would allow workers to specialize in one or two simple tasks that they could do quickly, without much training or education, and always with the same tools.

Even though the concept of an assembly line was well known, the technology to build and power such a plant was lacking. Moving a two-ton automobile on a conveyor belt was no simple feat. This is where Ford's years of experience at the Edison Illuminating Company gave him an advantage over the competition. As chief engineer at Edison, his work involved designing electric motors. Being the risk taker that he was, Henry Ford built a new and radically different production facility at Highland Park, Michigan. At its heart was a 3000 horsepower generator that provided electricity to motors powering conveyor belts, the line shafting and everything else in the factory. It was the world's first electrified assembly line.[2] Continuous mass production was born and the effects were astounding.

Prior to assembly production, the efficiency per employee was 8.306 automobiles per year. By 1915 it had increased to 20.8791, an efficiency increase of 150 percent in just two years. When the production results for 1914 were totalled, the

Ford Motor Company had built 308,162 Model T Fords, 56 percent of all the cars produced in the U.S. that year. Ford had also built more than half of the nation's new cars with just one-sixth of its automotive workforce. In fact, while production numbers went up, the actual number of workers employed by Ford went down. In 1915, 394,788 Model T Fords were produced.[3] This was an incredible increase of 312,400 automobiles over 1912 production levels.

Just as efficiency and output increased, so did profits. The net income of the Ford Motor Company went from $4 million in 1910 to $13.5 million in 1913. Henry Ford had become one of the richest and most famous men in the world.

This rapid growth in profitability quickly attracted the attention of the business community. Ford's electrified factory was making him a lot of money and many other businesses wanted a piece of the action. Companies across the US electrified their plants. Mass production techniques were applied to the production of sewing machines, lighting, furniture, radios, and virtually everything else. Electrified conveyor belts powered by generators drove an ever growing number of continuous production lines across the United States. Productivity rates in almost all sectors of the economy increased exponentially. On average, worker productivity between 1920 and 1929 rose 60 percent. By 1929, electric motors provided 78 percent of all mechanical drive.[4] Total electrical consumption in manufacturing increased six-fold between 1912 and 1930, (from 9,250 million kilowatts-hours to 53,930 million kilowatts-hours) Any factory that did not adapt and electrify its facilities was at a competitive disadvantage and was either forced to electrify or went bankrupt.

Electrifying a production line was not a cheap process and many factories had to borrow substantial amounts of money to make the transition. But with the great profits that the Ford Company and others were making, banks were eager to lend money.

It was not just factories that were caught up in the throes of the mass production revolution; it was also the agricultural sector. As factories turned out increasingly more wondrous and now affordable mechanization tools such as tractors and harvesters, farmers who adopted these new technologies were able to plough, plant and harvest more acreage with less labour. By 1929 there were five times as many tractors in use as in 1919.[5] The agricultural labour force was halved and then halved again. Millions of people in the early part of the twentieth century lost their jobs and flocked to the cities.

The Roaring Twenties were a period of rapid industrial growth for the United States. The factories were in overdrive, turning out cars, radios, toasters, sewing machines and a lot of other goods. The laissez-faire capitalism model, whose philosophy ruled the day, required only that government stay out of the affairs of corporations, something it seemed more than willing to do.

There was, however, one small problem. Even though the production capacity per worker in the United States had increased by approximately 60 percent between 1920 and 1929, Americans were not consuming all the goods being produced.[6] Warehouses were bloated, showroom floors were packed. Consumer spending was not able to keep up with production. Just as with Hargreaves' spinning jenny, the advances in industrial efficiency created a situation where the supply of goods and services exceeded demand.

This is the mandate of technology. The more efficient it makes us, the less labour is required to produce goods. Unless we consume more, we have a surplus in labour, people lose their jobs and we end up in a recession.

By 1927, car sales in the USA were in decline. In 1928, the US was in recession. In 1929 the stock market collapsed.

The abrupt unravelling of the tangled web of debt and speculation was spectacular. The problem was not just that people were losing their jobs. Banks and investors had lent out large sums of money on the speculation that factories and farms would capitalize on new production technologies. When profits did not materialize, farmers and investors could not meet their debt obligations. Companies began to go bankrupt and farmers lost their land. As more people defaulted on their loans, more banks declared bankruptcy. As more banks went bankrupt, more people lost their savings. The more people lost their jobs and savings, the less they could spend, and the less money consumers spent, the more companies went bankrupt. So the cycle continued.

This vicious cycle was aggravated when investment funds completely dried up. Investors were not interested in putting money into an economy that was contracting. As soon as hard times hit, investors saw no need to invest and financial liquidity in the markets evaporated. By 1933, unemployment

had increased to 25 percent and the economy had contracted by 33 percent over 1928 levels.

This was a perfect financial storm. The financial collapse of the economy is often blamed for the Great Depression. However, the financial collapse was an inevitable consequence of the economic collapse. The health of the financial system operates within the greater context of the health of the economy.

And that is the story of Henry Ford and the Great Depression. In general structure and development, it is entertainingly similar to Hargreaves and his spinning jenny. The only important difference seems to be that no Luddites appeared on the scene, attempting to turn back the wave of technological progress. Well, at least not at this time...

Notes:

1. Beaudreau, Bernard C. 1996. Authors Choice Press: Lincoln, NE. *Mass production, the Stock Market Crash, and the Great Depression: The Macroeconomics of Electrification.* ISBN: 0-595-32334-0. Page 18.

2. Ibid, page 5.

3. Ibid, page 7.

4. Ibid, page 12.

5. Alvord, Katie T. 2000. New Society Publishers. Divorce Your Car!: Ending the Love Affair with the Automobile. ISBN: 08-86571-408-8. Page 23.

6. Beaudreau, Bernard C. 1996. Authors Choice Press: Lincoln, NE. *Mass production, the Stock Market Crash, and the Great Depression: The Macroeconomics of Electrification.* ISBN: 0-595-32334-0. Page 17.

Chapter 4
The Architecture of Consumerism

Technology increases the efficiency with which we can produce goods and services. The more we can produce, the more we need to consume.

The fabulously efficient new machines and factories did not cause the Great Depression of the 1930s. Technology alone does not cause recessions. It simply puts a mandate on society to consume more. If that mandate is not met, if consumption does not increase, there will be a reduction in the amount of work available. Mass production needs to continuously be balanced with mass consumption. In a world of incredibly efficient machines, without mass production there will be mass unemployment.

During the Great Depression, consumption of goods and services did not increase at a rate commensurate to that of increased production. Why did consumers stop spending? How the mandate of consumerism was not met is a mystery whose solution still eludes many academics. To this day, there are many schools of thought with conflicting explanations as to the causes of the Great Depression. There is less disagreement that for the economy of the thirties to recover, people needed to go shopping and purchase all the products being produced.

For consumers to fulfill this dutiful task of consuming all the products being produced there were two necessary elements: people needed to be able to afford to buy more and even more importantly, they needed to want to buy more.

People Needed to Be Able to Afford to Buy More

New technological advances made Henry Ford one of the richest men in the US, but not all were equally blessed by this new found financial prosperity. Real wages only increased marginally. With new technology, workers could produce 60 percent more products between 1920 and 1929, but they could not afford to consume 60 percent more. The income-gap between the rich and the poor in the United States was at its widest level in modern history.[1]

Simply filling up showroom floors and warehouses with product is not enough. Mass consumption requires a consumer society both willing and able to go on a shopping spree. Shopping, as we all know, needs to be financed by either money or debt.

Since consumers and workers are essentially the same people, legislation was needed to ensure that workers got a bigger piece of the corporate profit pie. Edward Filene, an economist of the time, put it as follows: "The businessman of the future must fill the pockets of the workers and consumers before he can fill his pockets."[1]

Much of President Roosevelt's New Deal legislation served to achieve the financial empowerment of workers/consumers. Since this is a topic well debated in history books I am including only a short summary of this topic in appendix A.

People Needed to Want to Buy More

Our great-grandparents, and in some cases, our grandparents, had a very different perspective on the utility of goods than we have today. They were born prior to the age of mass production and their values reflect this. What possessions they had were often handmade and expensive, both in labour and money. Spoons, tools, clothes, furniture and indeed, buildings, were handed down from generation to generation. What was built was built to last and was carefully looked after. There was a certain pride in being able to build, mend and maintain whatever was needed. The ideas of disposable goods and built-in obsolescence were utterly alien to those earlier generations. What they were was frugal. What the wheels of industry needed was a wasteful, freewheeling attitude.

A writer of the time, Kenneth Burke, wrote a satirical article called "Waste, The Future of Prosperity."[2] The article's thesis maintained that the more we learn to use what we do not need, the greater our consumption. The greater our consumption, the greater our production; and the greater our production, the greater our prosperity. "By this system," Burke wrote, "business need never face a saturation point. For though there is a limit to what a man can use, there is no limit whatever to what he can waste." He added a sole proviso, "We have simply to make sure that the increase in the number of labour saving devices does not shorten the hours of labour."

Imagine his surprise when this piece of satire became one of the cornerstones of twentieth century economic growth. Twenty-six years later, Kenneth Burke quoted an article in Business Week magazine "Just past the mid mark of the twentieth Century it looks as though all of our business forces are bent on getting every one [and here is the notable slogan] to borrow. Spend. Buy. Waste. Want." Burke reflected, "I would then have looked upon such a slogan as ideal material for a farce. Now presumably it is to be taken in full earnest." [3]

The problem was not just one of stubbornness. At the beginning of the twentieth century, people literally needed less.

Automobile manufacturers of the era consumed 15 percent of all steel, half of all iron, 80 percent all rubber, 63 percent of all plate glass, 33 percent of all nickel, 14 percent of all cotton, 20 percent of all lumber and were the single biggest consumer of *date* coal. Just as it is today, the automobile sector directly and —— indirectly employed more people than any other. [4]

Even though automobiles were essential for the economy, they were non-essential items for citizens. Many cities had been designed and built mostly prior to the advent of mass production of the automobile. They were designed to facilitate the mobility of people, not cars. There were no highways or mass daily suburban commutes. People who worked in the city lived in the city. The baker, butcher and other small community mom-and-pop stores were in walking or cycling distance. Bicycles were also more popular. Around four million bicycles were used around North America.[5] For longer commutes, most large cities, including New York, Chicago, Philadelphia and Los Angeles, had effective inter-urban electric tram systems that allowed people to get from one end of the city to the next.

Those that did have cars found their utility lacking. By 1920, the number of cars had doubled but the number of roads had not. Congestion was a problem even then. The traffic speed on New York's Fifth Avenue was four miles per hour. There were also no interstate highways connecting various cities. The rural roads were mostly in poor condition and not conducive to automobile travel. The result was that by 1927 the demand for automobiles, the biggest engine of growth, was in decline.

Technology increases the efficiency with which we can produce products, but if people do not need to consume more, it also means less labour is required. As car sales declined, so did employment and income earned, not just of those manufacturing automobiles, but also for workers in all the ancillary industries; from iron mining to cotton picking.

The 1920s and 30s were a time of different values and needs. The frugal values of our great-grandparents were not conducive to a culture of mass consumption. Cities were not built around self-contained neighbourhoods that made the automobile, the prime engine of growth, the essential item it is today.

For the United States to recover from the Depression the incredibly efficient factories needed a more needy and wasteful society. Mass production had been invented and the economy collapsed. A sister technology was required: the social technology of consumerism.

As it turned out, mass production was easier to invent than consumerism. President Roosevelt understood the need for mass consumption, but he had no clear vision on how to create a culture of consumers. His work centred around empowering citizens financially and protecting them from unethical business practices.

Despite the lack of a clear vision, Roosevelt laid the groundwork, or better yet, the road work for one of the central pillars for the emergence of a consumer culture: suburbia. Part of the president's industrial recovery plan was to hire thousands of workers to build roads. By 1939, vast networks of roads crisscrossed the country. Where roads went, suburban developments became possible. The potential for development made the emergence of a consumer culture possible. Roads, suburbs, malls and millions of new cars were just a few years away.

President Roosevelt died in 1945. Even though he did not live to see the emergence of modern day consumer culture, he did live to see a form of consumerism: World War II. There are few things in this world more capable of employing resources than war. War creates an instant demand for guns, bullets, tanks, bombs and planes. In a short space of time, idle American factories were back to peak production. Americans were back to work, either manufacturing the tools of war or using them.

World War II temporarily marked the end of the Great Depression.

Notes:

1. Beaudreau, Bernard C. 1996. Authors Choice Press: Lincoln, NE. *Mass production, the Stock Market Crash, and the Great Depression: The Macroeconomics of Electrification.* ISBN: 0-595-32334-0. Page 21.

2. Henry M Christman. A View of the Nation: An Anthology. ISBN: 9780836916201. Page 210

3. ibid

4. *The Triumph of America 1933*. Produced by Jam Handy. This film can be viewed at www.EfficiencyShifting.com

5. Alvord, Katie T. 2000. New Society Publishers. *Divorce Your Car!: Ending the Love Affair with the Automobile.* ISBN: 08-86571-408-8. Page 25.

Chapter 5
Consumerism at Last

In 1945, the Second World War came to an end. First, Germany surrendered in May and then Japan on August 15th. The war had lasted just over five years. During this time the American economy had produced more tanks, planes, ships and wartime products than all the other nations combined, including both Allied and Axis nations. The term 'American Made' had an entirely different meaning and respect in those days. American industrial might had dwarfed Germany, Italy and Japan. The American factories that once lay idle, had become its biggest asset.[1]

With the war over, millions of soldiers were returning home and their future was uncertain. Many, including Roosevelt were concerned that without American factories producing huge amounts of wartime products, the economy would return to its pre-war state of depression.

The challenge and focus for Roosevelt, and then President Truman, became to keep the economy functioning and find work for the returning GIs. Despite the gloomy outlook, something had changed. Over a generation had passed since the beginning of the Great Depression and the returning soldiers had a very different perspective on life and values.

The majority of returning soldiers had come from rural America, a hard and isolated existence. Farm hours were long, for little pay and, except for church on Sundays and harvest fest, were dull. To returning soldiers who had now traveled the world and seen different cities, city life had more appeal. What they wanted was girls, parties and careers. To help train and accommodate the aspirations of the returning GIs, President Roosevelt, introduced the GI Bill. This bill is often regarded as the last piece of legislature of the New Deal.

The GI Bill provided college or vocational training for returning World War II veterans. 7.8 million took advantage of the opportunities the bill offered. It also provided low interest and zero down payment loans for servicemen to purchase homes. The majority of the new homes purchased were in the newly created world of affordable suburbia.[2]

2.4 million returning GIs purchased these new homes.[3] Unlike apartment city dwellers, suburbanites were very dependent on automobiles. Cars were needed to get to work, go shopping and visit relatives. The automobile, the biggest engine of growth in the US was in demand again. Millions of cars were sold.

Automobiles were not the only items on the shopping list of the newly emerging consumerist culture. New suburban homes did not have the same space restrictions as tiny city apartments. Suburban homes had space for washing machines, lawn mowers, kids' rooms filled with toys, television sets (from 1947) and garages filled with tools for the handyman.

Returning war veterans were also keen to get married and have children. Returning soldiers marked the beginning of the baby boom. Between 1942 and 1953 an estimated 77.3 million babies were born. Babies that needed diapers, toys and later their own cars and houses. [4]

By the 1950s, the United States' role as a world leader had been secured. As a result of increased efficiency, the American worker could produce in an hour more than six times more goods and services than the average Japanese worker and over twice as much as French workers.

Television sets were introduced in 1947, but the relationship between Americans and their televisions really started to blossom in the fifties. Between 1954 and 1956, approximately 10,000 television sets were sold every day[5]. The most popular television show was *Leave It To Beaver*. It was a family-oriented situation comedy about an inquisitive, but often naïve, boy named Theodore "Beaver" Cleaver and his adventures at home, in school, and around his suburban neighbourhood.

The show gained iconic status, with the Cleavers exemplifying the idealized suburban family of the mid-twentieth century. Mom stayed home in her apron while Dad went to his white-collar job, coming home every night to a hot dinner. The kids were lovable scamps who were always getting into 'scrapes' of one kind or another and had to be straightened out by the wisdom dispensed by Dad as he smoked his pipe.

Every night, millions of American families would sit down in front of their television sets and watch the news, comedies, dramas and, of course, many hours of advertising for cigarettes, toy guns, washing powder and, most significantly, automobiles. In 1956, the largest individual advertising budgets were Chevrolet ($30.4 million), Ford ($25 million), followed by Buick, Dodge, Plymouth, Mercury, Chrysler, Pontiac and Oldsmobile. Only Coca-Cola, at $10.9 million, broke into the top ten Detroit hegemony. Motor vehicle registration leaped from \$31 million in 1945 to \$73.8 million fifteen years later.[6]

Unlike in years prior to the Great Depression, the government was well aware of the need to foster consumerism. According to the Chair of President Eisenhower's Council of Economic Advisors, "The American economy's ultimate purpose is to produce more consumer goods."[7]

The economist and retail analysis Victor Lebow summarized this in the following manner:

> Our enormously productive economy demands that we make consumption our way of life, that we convert the buying and use of goods into rituals, that we seek our spiritual satisfactions, our ego satisfactions, in consumption. The measure of social status, of social acceptance, of prestige, is now to be found in our consumptive patterns. The very meaning and significance of our lives today expressed in consumptive terms. The greater the pressures upon the individual to conform to safe and accepted social standards, the more does he tend to express his aspirations and his individuality in terms of what he wears, drives, eats - his home, his car, his pattern of food serving, his hobbies.[8]

President Eisenhower and his government delivered on this message with a new vision for the United States. Increasingly, American cities would become built around the automobile. The popular electric tram systems, which had previously made cars less of a necessity, were rapidly dismantled to make way for a new age of auto dependency. In 1956 the National Interstate and Defence Highways Act was signed into law. It was the biggest construction project in the history of the United States. At 40 acres per mile, 41,000 miles of new highway consumed over 1.6 million acres of land, most of which was purchased from farmers. Construction of the interstate system removed 42 billion cubic yards of earth, more than any other engineering project anywhere in the world at any time in history. Each mile of the system cost an average one million dollars. Billions of tons of steel, sand and cement were used. So many engineers were needed that, for the first time, state road departments hired female engineers. There were 54,663 bridges and 104 tunnels built in the system.

After he signed the Interstate law, Eisenhower said, "More than any single action by government … this one would change the face of America … Its impact on the American economy, the jobs it would produce in manufacturing and construction, the rural areas it would open up was beyond calculation". [9] Where the highway went, new suburban developments grew and cemented the automobile as an essential tool.

Consumer demand for suburban homes, cars and consumer goods to put in those homes kept American industry running at close to full employment. Consumerism was evolving to ensure that efficiency gains in industry would not result in higher unemployment and a repeat of the Great Depression.

In post-war America the second part of the puzzle of the Great Depression was being solved. Two components were needed. The first was the empowerment of consumers. This was accomplished by unions and NIRA. The second was that Americans needed to want to consume more. American thriftiness, the curse that had helped stall the factories needed to give way to a spending spree.

Consumerism was the solution to the Great Depression.

Notes:

1. Smith, Jean Edward. 2007. Random House: New York, NY. *FDR*. ISBN-10: 1400061210. Page 572.

2. One of the most significant components of President Roosevelt's New Deal was to employ thousands of Americans building roads. By 1939, vast networks of roads criss crossed the country. Where the roads went, suburban developments became possible.

3. Biggs, Selden and Biggs Helms, Lelia. 2007. M.E. Sharpe Inc.: Armonk, NY. *The Practice of American Public Policymaking*. ISBN 10: 0-7656-1775-7. Page 403.

4. Goldsmith, Jeff Charles. 2008. The Johns Hopkins University Press: Baltimore, MD. *The Long Baby Boom: An Optimistic Vision For a Graying Generation*. Page 11.

5. Winograd, Morley and Hais, Michael D. 2008. Rutgers University Press. *Millennial Makeover: MySpace, YouTube, and the Future of American Politics*. ISBN-10: 0813543010. Page 61.

6. Fox, Stephen R. 1997. University of Illinois Press. *The Mirror Makers: A History of American Advertising and Its Creators*. ISBN-10: 0252066596. Page 173.

7. Reich, Robert B. 1992. Vintage. *The Work of Nations: Preparing Ourselves for 21st Century Capitalism*. ISBN-10: 0679736158. Page 44.

8. Alan Thein Durning . How much is enough?: the consumer society and the future of the earth. Page 21

9. Carlos A. Schwantes. *Going places: transportation redefines the twentieth-century West.* ISBN 0-253-34202-3. Page 287

Chapter 6
Conclusion

The Great Depression is an important case study because we are witnessing the initial origins of twentieth century consumer culture. It provides an opportunity to analyze the architecture and, more importantly, the mechanics of consumerism.

The predominant view of consumerism is that it is simply us, the ever-lusting consumers, who want an endless amount of stuff. It is indeed true that we want to buy all the products being produced, but it is not the reason why we have to.

If consumerism were simply an issue of citizen desire, then all would be okay if we stopped buying and wasting. But it isn't. If consumers stop spending, the economy collapses and people lose their jobs. To make matters worse for politicians, restless unemployed citizens have a long history of getting rid of their failed political representatives. [1]

We are clearly stuck in a cycle and that cycle is the balancing of the increasing levels of efficiency with increasing levels of consumption.

The motive of James Hargreaves and Henry Ford was profit, just as with all corporations. Technology that increases efficiency means that with less labour they can produce more. Lower costs mean a healthier bottom line.

The next step is to get consumers to buy more. This is the task of corporations, government and us, the consumers. For corporations, the tool is advertising. Six hundred and fifty three billions dollars persuading us to need.[2]

For government, the tools vary from fiscal policy and urban planning to tax incentives. The role of government in enabling this cycle is probably more important than the role of corporations, but it is less deliberate and, more often than not, simply limited to ensuring that citizens have the ability to go shopping. For us, the consumers, our role is to have some level of trust in the status quo images that the media present us. If we had no trust in advertising, then consumerism would be a hard sell.

Regardless of whether consumer demand is a consequence of advertising, natural desire or deliberate government policies, increasing levels of efficiency need to be balanced with increasing levels of consumerism.

One way to look at the relationship between efficiency and consumer demand is that of a push pull relationship. Consumer demand pulls products through the system. Increasing levels of efficiency push and insist that products make it through the system.[3]

From the perspective of ecological sustainability, the issue of efficiency is of greater importance than consumer desire for products. As long as there is an increasing level of efficiency as a result of technological innovation, consumers will have little option other than to go shopping.

Notes:

1. A good example of political instability in a depression is the Great Depression. The Great Depression saw the rise of fascism in Italy, Spain and Germany. It also saw the rise of communism and escalating levels of social unrest in the United States.

2. In 2008 six hundred and fifty three billion dollars was spent world wide on advertising.

Jack W. Plunkett. Plunkett's Advertising and Branding Industry Almanac 2009.

3. This relationship applies to all manufactured products. It does not matter if the product is a new invention unlike anything before. An example of this is the steam engine and spinning jenny. Without the textile industry becoming more efficient, it would have been impossible to mass produce the steam engine. The efficiency gains in the textile industry freed up labour so that it could be employed else where. If making clothes and growing crops still constituted sufficient industry to create full employment, then there would not have been enough of a labour resource to mine iron, coal and manufacture the machines of the steam age.

PART 2
Automation and the Internet

The wheels of innovation rarely stop. Provided consumption increases, the end result is growth. The more efficient technology makes us, the more we can produce with less labour. Our ability to impact the ecology is greater than ever before.

With the spinning jenny and the assembly lines, society politically, culturally and economically evolved to consume more. The technologies that followed would have similar effects. Automation, computers and the internet would put the same mandate on society. The more efficient industry becomes, the more we have to evolve into a consumer culture.

Chapter 7
Automation

The march towards increasing levels of industrial efficiency did not end with electrification. It was, in fact, only in its beginning stages. In the 1950s a new technology was emerging that would have an equally profound effect on the evolution of consumer culture: automation.

Industrial automation was different from assembly lines and electrification. Assembly lines moved products through the factory to different work stations. Automation replaced the workers at the stations with machines. Computers connected to a series of logic units could be used to program machines to do certain tasks that were once done by humans.

As usual, Ford was at the leading edge of this new technology. One of the first places to implement the new automation technologies was the Brook Park Engine Plant. Ben Seligman, a Union of Auto Workers (UAW) analyst, described the automated operation of the 1500 foot long battery of machines: "Automatic machine and tools perform more than 500 boring, broaching, drilling, honing, milling, and tapping operations without any human assistance." On this automated machining line there were "less men . . . than formerly. In one part of the line 25 men perform the same as 117 did using the old method, mainly because it is no longer necessary to stand before each machine and accurately position the work before the machine tools can do the job." [1]

Even though automation technology was still in its infancy the effects were dramatic. In 1955, US Steel began the process of automating its production facilities. Between 1956 and 1961 production increased by 120 percent, while the work force decreased by 95,000 workers. Other industries experienced similar increases in output and profit. The United Auto Workers Union reported a loss of 160,000 members, while the Union of Electricians reported a loss of 80,000. Between 1956 and 1962 approximately 1.5 million people lost their jobs in manufacturing due to automation.[2]

The following story's authenticity is uncertain, but it is interesting nonetheless. One day Henry Ford was taking UAW President Walter Reuther on a tour of a new automated Ford project that had replaced all the workers with mechanical robots that busily assembled cars on the line. As he proudly walked along, Ford remarked to Reuther, "Well, Walter, how are you going to get these robots to go out on strike?" And Reuther shot back, "Well, Henry, how are you going to get these robots to buy Fords?"

In the 1960s, computers made their historic debut on the factory floor. Machines that were once dependent on the skills of their operators were now dependent on a switchable programmable card that controlled every minute function. The more sophisticated and cheaper computers became, the more skilled positions became redundant.

The cost savings from automation were significant. General Electric saw its earnings swell 21 percent to $242.5 million in 1962. When Smith-Corona Marchant (makers of typewriters and small computers) automated its assembly lines, profits went up 147 percent in two years. The best gains were in the oil industry, where machines, for the first time, ran entire refineries and petrochemical plants. Profits for Jersey

Standard, Texaco, Standard of Indiana and Mobile were all up. "Staff reduction is primarily responsible," said senior vice president George James of Socony Mobil, "We have been carrying on an intensive job method study, then offering early retirement plans wherever we can weed out unneeded workers." [3]

Even though automation made many workers redundant, as long as consumers kept on spending, the economy continued to grow and new jobs were created. Automation actually created jobs at Smith-Corona Marchant because the company had to hire more workers to handle its increased business but, says a spokesman, "We would have had to hire one-third more people than we actually did in order to get the same production using our old methods."

Me and Automation

In the 1990s I became intricately involved in the world of factory automation. I joined a large American multinational corporation called Rockwell Automation. I was a software engineer and my job was to write software that interfaced human operators and machines. The technical term was HMI (human machine interface) software. The software that I worked on controlled approximately 80 percent of all the factories in the United States, factories that made cigarettes, cars, steel, televisions, toys, cutlery and pretty much everything else. It was an interesting time in my life. I was at the heart of the supply side of the economy. People that know me today are surprised to hear that I used to have a regular nine to five job. I was sitting in a little grey cubicle playing with occasionally amusing software algorithms, but mostly working on my first book, *Workers of the World Relax*.

Business was booming for Rockwell Automation. The more corporations realized the profit potential of replacing humans with machines, the more automation equipment we sold. The MIT Sloan School of Management published productivity data collected over a five-year period, from 1987 to 1991, for more than 380 giant firms. The study found that the return on investment for manufacturing and services was 68 percent.[4] In 1980, United States Steel, the largest integrated steel company in the US, employed 120,000 workers. By 1990 it was producing roughly the same output using only 20,000. General Electric, the world's largest corporation, has reduced worldwide employment from 400,000 in 1981 to less than 230,000 in 1993, while tripling its sales. These numbers are projected to fall even further in the coming decades.

In 1980, ten billion dollars of automation products (robots and software) were sold. By 1986, it was 18 billion dollars. By 2004, it was a 50 billion dollar market, growing at a rate of 6.4 percent per year. Market share for the product I worked on had grown 150 percent in the late nineties. The team I worked with was tasked with implementing the distributed architecture of the software. Essentially, this allowed a group of managers to run and control almost every aspect of production from an office thousands of miles away. If the software was implemented correctly, on-site managers became redundant.

It sounds impressive, but its construction quality was incredibly poor. Though it did the job, if customers ever found out that the only way we were able to get it to work using the internet was to bypass all the network security, they would have sued us. I remember watching the two planes fly into the Twin Towers and thinking, if the terrorists only knew that they could shut have down a substantial amount of US industry by simply typing a few small commands from any internet browser in the world. [5]

My skills and training were in automation software development. In essence, I made my living by making other people's jobs unnecessary. My interests, however, were in trying to understand the connectivity between the economy, the people and the machines.

It was not a clear-cut ethical issue. For many factories and businesses in the US, Canada and Europe, automation was the only way they could stay in business. In the world of free trade, increasing numbers of firms were moving their plants where labour was cheaper: sweatshops in Guatemala, programmers who worked seven days a week in China, skilled labour in India that worked for an eighth of US wages. Unskilled and skilled labour was becoming increasingly cheap as nations competed to attract foreign investment. The only way a factory in Europe, Canada or the US could remain competitive was to have machines that were willing to work for even less than sweatshop wages.

Who Would Become Redundant?

When a firm automated, who became redundant had a lot to do with the evolution of computers. In the fifties, computers were huge machines that could take up entire rooms and swallowed up large budgets. As they became smaller, faster and more intelligent, their evolution moved through the factory floor. Initially, it was the least skilled employees that were replaced. Tasks that were repetitive and boring were the easiest to automate.

In the United States, the least skilled employees were African Americans. Years of racist educational policies had delegated them to the simplest tasks. Even though there was not a recession in the fifties and sixties, increasing numbers of African Americans were finding themselves without jobs. An urban African American poverty problem resulted. Nowhere was it more significant than in Detroit, the home of GM, Chrysler and Ford. In the forties and fifties, Detroit had become the fourth largest city in the US and one of the fastest growing. The auto factories recruited Americans regardless of race. There seemed to be no end to the amount of work needed to fill American highways and suburbs with cars. From the 1950s onwards, however, these employment opportunities evaporated as factories automated. Even though production was on the rise, employment (especially for the unskilled) was declining. As of April 2009, unemployment in Detroit stood at 22 percent. Many African American communities have been living in a depression for a long time.

The effect of rising unemployment in the automotive sector as a result of automation is a problem that the Union of Auto Workers has been well aware of. In 1955, the UAW issued a resolution at its annual general convention stating that "The UAW welcomes automation [and] technological progress... We offer our cooperation...in a common search for policies and programs...that will insure that greater technological progress will result in greater human progress." [6]

Union members believed that provided there were training opportunities, displaced workers would be able to find new, more rewarding jobs. The opposite happened. It was computers that were becoming more intelligent, affordable and efficient. The more sophisticated they became, the more job positions became redundant. Initially, it was the unskilled that were made redundant. In the 1980s, with the advent of the personal computer, lower and then middle management would be next on the chopping block.

Notes:

1. Meyer, Steve, "'An Economic "Frankenstein"': UAW Workers' Responses to Automation at the Ford Brook Park Plant in the 1950s," *Michigan Historical Review,* 28 (Spring 2002), 63–89.

2. Rifkin, Jeremy. 2004. Tarcher. *The End of Work.* ISBN-10: 1585423130. Page 67.

3. Time Magazine. Feb 9, 1962. *State of Business: Automation's Dividends.* Retrieved from: http://www.time.com.

4. Rifkin, Jeremy. 2004. Tarcher. *The End of Work.* ISBN-10: 1585423130. Page 92.

5. The situation was even worse than this: not only did the software not have any effective security, but there was also no way any reliable security could be built into the system. Once the programming code was written it was shipped off to China to be maintained and upgraded by programmers who were willing to work for a third of the wage. The HMI software that we wrote controlled not only factories but many military facilities. From a security perspective this is quite amazing. Any semiskilled hacker could shut down a sizable majority of American industry. Even if a security patch were made, it would be compiled and shipped from

China. This is all information I know because I wrote parts of this programming code.

6. Rifkin, Jeremy. 2004. Tarcher. *The End of Work.* ISBN-10: 1585423130. Page 85.

Chapter 8
Computers and the Internet

Computers

The clever machines of automation made simple human tasks redundant. Initially, it was manual labour positions that machines would replace. Repetitive jobs, tasks that required less thinking were the first for machines to take over. Cheap affordable computers would change this. As the technology evolved, so too would the complexity of tasks that machines could perform.

In the 1980s, American businesses invested more than one trillion dollars in information technology. A computer with the right kind of software is essentially an entire roomful of managers in a box. Highly complex skills, that would previously have required a team of well-educated college graduates, are now neatly packed into a software algorithm. The skills of a credit manager evaluating customers' credit risk, honed over years of experience, could now be activated by simply pressing the space bar. The inventory stock levels in a warehouse or store miles away could be displayed in seconds on a screen. Invoices and other mail-outs are done with a few clicks on a keyboard. Purchasing, credit and inventory managers who thought their jobs were secure now found themselves in a precarious position.

One of the first companies to harness the potentials of computers and remote connectivity was the American retail giant Walmart. In 1983, Walmart became the first company to introduce electronic scanners connected to a central database at the sales registers. Each time a sale was made, inventory levels would be automatically updated. A computer located at head office could recognize when inventory levels were low, put in a purchase order request, and automatically ship merchandise from a warehouse. Gone were the days of managers manually counting inventory, filling out reams of paperwork and requesting shipments that would arrive months after an item was out of stock. Wal-Mart was also the first company to set up a satellite network that provided two-way voice and video communication between stores. It went so far as to set up a tracking system on trucks so that loading crews would know exactly when a truck was to arrive.

The technological efficiency that Wal-Mart embraced gave the company a cost advantage over its competitors. That's the Wal-Mart business philosophy, to lower running costs so it can offer cheaper prices and thus have bigger sales. With everything managed by head office or automatically, fewer on-site managers were needed. More and larger stores connected through a centralized computer network also gave Wal-mart the ability to gain economies of scale. The more stores it had, the bigger the discounts it could negotiate from suppliers.

Information technology made Wal-Mart more efficient than its competitors. On the surface, a win-win situation: customers get cheap products and Wal-Mart makes lots of profit. It did not take long for many other stores to recognize the efficiency advantages that were making Wal-Mart such a success. Soon Kmart, Target, Office Max, PetSmart, Superstore and Toys "R" Us followed the efficiency recipe. Without computers, none of these megastores would have been possible. Computers make more sales possible with less labour.

One 1999 study reported that 1.5 jobs had been lost for every job that Wal-Mart created. A recent projection by the University of Illinois at Chicago's Center for Urban Economic Development concluded that a proposed West-Side Chicago Wal-Mart would likely yield a net decrease of about 65 jobs if it opened.[1]

It was not just Wal-Mart and other big-box stores that were benefiting from efficiencies that computers introduced. The benefits extended to every business that utilized them. From travel agents that no longer needed to make phone calls around the globe, to stock exchange traders tracking billions of transactions, computers added efficiencies throughout the economy.

The Internet

The growth of the internet gave the efficiency of computers another productivity boost. Thanks to the internet, it became much easier for retailers to order directly from manufacturers around the world. In 1992 alone, the wholesale sector lost 69,000 jobs.[2]

Technologies such as the spinning jenny, the assembly line, the computer and the internet make industry more efficient. The more efficient industry becomes, the more can be produced and sold with less labour. Provided that people consume more, there is no net reduction in employment.[3] The evolution of the internet would make this a whole lot more complicated.

The effects of computers and the internet would not be isolated to the productive sector of the economy. In our personal lives there would be an even more significant effect. Close to where I live there is a little independent video store. It carries a fair mix of Hollywood blockbuster films and alternative foreign and local films. Despite being one of the most popular stores in the neighbourhood its sales are down. It used to have a busy staff of four, now there is only the owner, trying desperately to keep the store from going under.

What happened to his business is the internet. A new release in his store is $5.50. If you download the film using a shareware program such as LimeWire or BitTorrent you can get the film for free months before it is released on DVD. Best of all, you get to keep the movie and there are no late fees. Universal Studios and Disney have embarked on a million dollar advertising campaign to try and convince people that downloading a film is unethical and the same thing as stealing. The strategy is not working for the movie industry any more than it did for the music industry. I suspect that the idea of stealing from firms such as Disney, Fox and Universal adds to the appeal of downloading.

If you open up your internet browser and search any topic, the odds are you will find a million passionate people taking pride in that topic. The mainstream presence that exists on the internet is virtually all free. I can click on BBC, the Guardian, CNN, the New York Times and get any news I want for free. It's free because if it weren't, I would simply choose other news service that was free. The effects on news publication profit margins are devastating. The San Francisco Chronicle is losing one million dollars a week.[4] The Washington Post, one of the most stable American papers, reported a 77 percent drop in earnings in the fourth quarter of 2008. In 2008, the Chicago Sun Times stocks were booted off the NYSE as worthless.[5] In March of 2009, the Seattle Post-Intelligencer ceased hard copy publication altogether after 146 years and is now only available on the internet. The New York Daily News, Los Angeles Times, St. Paul Pioneer Press and Detroit News are all in financial trouble.

Television stations are faring no better. Revenue declined by 13 percent in 2008. CBS Corporation announced a net income loss of $11.8 billion for 2008, a 52 percent fall. Fox TV is expecting a $1.16 billion loss in revenue. According to BIA Advisory Services, TV station revenues for 2009 will decline 17.3 percent from 2008 levels. Auto advertising on TV stations declined by more than $900 million in 2008. The world of television, just like newspapers, is a world in trouble. Station such as ABC, CBC, News Corp and City TV that helped define the consumer spending culture, might disappear.

The hopes that the internet might become a new media force to inspire consumer spending are also not being fulfilled. Even though millions of people are turning to sites such as Craigslist and eBay, most of the stuff they are buying is second hand. I recently had the great joy of becoming a father. In January 2008, my little baby boy Mika came into the world. One of my initial concerns was how I was going to afford all the things a little baby needs. The solution was Craigslist. Toys, cribs, jumpers, swings, bicycle seats, strollers, shoes, clothes and books - it's all there. And as soon as he outgrows something, we simply put it back on Craigslist and somebody else picks it up. The net effect is that a community of sharing is created. The more we share, the less gets manufactured, and of course, the less people are employed in manufacturing. The site statistics on Craigslist are incredible. Every month approximately 50 million new ads are placed, and it gets about 20 billion hits per day. EBay gets similarly impressive statistics. The end result is my baby boy and me are happy, and the ecosystem is better off, but it does raise concern about what we do with all the excess industrial efficiencies in the system.

The technology of the internet is similar in effect to Henry Ford's assembly lines, the spinning jenny and automation. The difference is that even though it helps industry produce more products, it makes it difficult to balance increased production with increased consumption.

Consumerism needs a society of people who don't share, people who waste and eagerly turn to newspapers and television to find out what the newest must-have items are.

The internet is changing this. The newspapers and television, along with their adverts that have helped inspire so much consumption over the past century, are disappearing. In their place is a tool that enables people to communicate and share.

The ramifications are still in their early stages, but clearly there is a paradigm shift at hand.

Notes:

1. Moberg, David: InTheseTimes.com. June 10, 2004. *The Wal-Mart Effect The hows and whys of beating the Bentonville behemoth.* Retrieved from: http://www.inthesetimes.com/article/the_wal_mart_effect/.

2. Rifkin, Jeremy. 2004. Tarcher. The End of Work. ISBN-10: 1585423130. Page 152.

3. Mass production requires mass consumption. The two always need to be balanced. If output increases by 3%, consumption needs to increase by 3%. Increased consumption may be in the form of disposable coffee cups, new computers, more airplane flights, new cars, or a super yacht for a billionaire. There are many ways consumption of products can be increased. It could be a government decision to build more roads or to increase military spending in a war. It could be a management decision in the form of earlier built-in product obsolescence. It could be consumers simply deciding that they absolutely must have a new skin toner, shampoo, or some other beauty product. How consumption increases to match productivity is not as important as that it does. The jobs lost as a result of increased efficiency need to be made up in the form of new jobs created elsewhere.

4. New York Times. Richard Perez. Papers Facing Worst Year for Ad Revenue. June 23, 2008

5. Associated Press, Chicago Sun-Times sale to investor group finalized. Oct 26, 2009

Chapter 9
World Wide Financial Crisis

Between 2000 and 2008, American productivity grew on average by 3.3 percent annualy.[1] With less labour, Americans could produce more. Consumption of goods did not increase proportionately and employment rates declined.[2] In 2007, the American economy went into recession. In 2008, the economies of most of the rest of the world followed. The economy contracted more than at any time since the Great Depression. There were many explanations as to the causes. The predominant theory was that the American housing market was loaded with toxic debt. [3]

Another explanation was that capitalism had drained the consumer purchasing power of the economy.[4] There was also the view that a level of market saturation had been reached and consumers simply did not want or need another car, a third television and a second cell phone for the year.[5] Even present day consumer culture theoretically must have limits. All these explanations to varying degrees have credible aspects, but they ignore the most fundamental question: why is it that we are stuck in this cycle of contently trying to match increased consumption to increased production? Why is it that the economy has to grow and we have to consistently go shopping in order to avoid massive unemployment? What needs to be addressed is how technological efficiency puts a mandate on society. The more efficient industry becomes the more society is forced to evolve to increasing levels of consumerism. The reason for the failure of society to meet the mandate is a separate topic to the mandate itself.

In May 2009, I bumped into an old friend of mine, Stoo Abraham, and he told me that he and the rest of the automation development staff at Rockwell were all about to be laid off. The offices were to be shutdown in one week's time. I decided to attend that last day.

There were tears, and even a few happy moments, as all the employees packed their belongings into little boxes and left the building. The most tears came from my friend Evana. She had been there 15 years and has always been a good, patient person, provided that nobody was cooking popcorn in the office. She hates the smell of popcorn.

I could not help but think of how technology had come full circle. Back in the initial days of automation many had hoped that, through retraining, those whose jobs had been made redundant could move up the skill and income ladder into more rewarding careers.

The automation engineers were at the top of that career food chain. It was their skills and innovations that created the machines and software that ran them. No job should have been more secure. Yet here they were, unemployed, themselves being made redundant. How could this be?

What had happened was that orders for new robots, PLC (Program Logic Controls) and other components had dried up. As factories across the world downsized to deal with shrinking markets, they no longer had the money or the need to invest in new equipment. The dream of workers being retrained and moving into new higher paying and challenging careers did not happen. Fewer workers were needed to make all the products being manufactured.

Just as the UAW president said in that fabled conversation with Henry Ford, "but Henry, how are you going to get all these machines to buy Fords?" The machines and robots could not buy more cars. The clever computers running the accounting, doing credit checks and sending out bills could not go shopping at Walmart.

The cheap labourers working in sweatshops in Honduras, Guatemala or Mexico were also in no position to buy 40 inch televisions nor hybrid Fords or even Nike running shoes, for that matter.

Automation, ICs and the internet has increased our capacity to produce more goods than we can consume. Just as during the Great Depression, the showroom floors and warehouses were loaded to the rafters. Just as during the Great Depression, politicians and economists now needed to once again find new ways to encourage consumers to go shopping and empower them to do so.

Mass production always needs to be balanced by mass consumption. What is needed to rescue the economy is a new form of even more intense consumerism. Are we doomed to have to shop our way through every economic slowdown?

The ecological toll of all this manufacturing, consumption and disposal is affecting the ecological sustainability of the planet. Climate change and species extinction rates are becoming hard to deny.

What we are dealing with is two crises: an economy that is slowing down and an ecosystem in distress. According to the UN, Obama and most leaders around the world, the solution to both these crises is green consumerism or, as the UN calls it, green growth.

Just as in the past, the Pandora's box of technology will be opened and there will be a few unexpected consequences.

Notes:

1. United Bureau of Statistics, News Release, USDL-09-1330

2. United Bureau of Statistics, Table 1. Employment status of the civilian noninstitutional population, 1940 to date

3. The easiest way to describe the toxic debt problem of the American banking system is to see it as two separate issues. One, large amounts of loans were improperly given higher credit ratings (implying lower risk of default). The second is that the value of the homes securing these loans has dropped.

In a normal time period, when a homeowner defaulted on the loan, the home itself could be resold to recoup the loss. With millions of homes now worth less, there is no collateral to restore the debt holders. It's what makes this debt "toxic."

4. Henry Ford, President Roosevelt and many others believed that one of the major contributors to the Great Depression was the growing divide between the rich and the poor. The consequence was that citizens no longer had the financial means to purchase the products that they were producing.

When throwing his support behind the National Industrial Recovery Act of 1933, Ford declared: We've got to stop that gouging process if we want to see all of the people reasonably prosperous. There is only one rule for industrialists and that is: Make the best quality of goods possible at the lowest cost paying the highest wages possible. Nothing can be right in this country until wages are right. The

life of business comes forth from the people in orders. The factories are not stopped for the lack of money, but the lack of orders. Money loaned at the top means nothing. Money spent at the bottom starts everything."

Much of the legislation in the National Industrial Recovery Act sought to address this imbalance.

From the 1970s onwards there was a gradual move back to laissez faire capitalism. Much of the legislation of the National Industrial Recovery Act has been revoked and or lapsed. In addition liberal trade agreements between nations contributes to this problem by again creating a global work force that can't earn enough money to buy the products that they are manufacturing. In essence, the major causes of the Great Depression have been replicated on a global scale.

As a result of a move to new conservative economics and the liberalization of trade agreements between nations, there is an inequality

5. The first sign of trouble in the economy was the failing auto sector. For some, the auto sector is a bit like the 'canary in the coal mine'. For others the auto sector is the coal mine. According to the American Automobile Association, one in seven jobs are related to the auto sector. It's more than just cars. It's mines that mine steel, it's companies that make tires, it's cities that build highways, it's police officers that give out speeding tickets.

The Worlds Largest Automaker of the Century GM, has not made a profit since 2004. The entire American auto sector had been in trouble for quite sometime. In 2006 GM, Ford, and Chrysler declined by 8.7%, 8%, and 7%, respectively. A significant decline. They continued their declines in 2007, 2008 and of course 2009.

This pattern was very similar to that of the Great Depression. Car sales in the 1920s had peaked in 1927, approximately two years before the collapse of Wall Street in 1929.

PART 3
Green Efficiency

The first and second part of this book dealt with the effects of increased efficiency in industry.

The third part of this book deals with the effects of increased efficiency on the ecology.

Chapter 10
A Green New Deal

President Roosevelt (1933)

President Barack Obama (2009)

During a time of uncertainty and financial disaster, when the bedrock of American society appeared to be crumbling, a man came forward onto the stage of national politics. His words and ideas connected with the common man. He offered a calm reassurance that America would shrug off its woes and move forward to a dazzling future.

In 1932, President Franklin Roosevelt faced civil unrest and massive unemployment. The Depression pounded all stimulants out of the economy, repelled investors, companies and workers. The United States was in a desperate situation. Roosevelt decided to increase government spending to a level previously unseen, to put people to work building vast projects that would create or improve infrastructure and in turn spur more jobs and growth: the New Deal.

In 2009 President Barack Obama offered American citizens a new New Deal, this time a green one. Instead of Roosevelt's huge dams and tunnels, Obama promised, "jobs that cannot be outsourced. Jobs building solar panels, wind turbines, constructing fuel efficient cars and buildings and developing the new energy efficient technologies that will lead to even more jobs."[1]

Barack Obama rose to the presidency on the power of hope and the promise of a new era in America. He now offers a plan that will fix the economy and save the world from impending environmental ruin. Parts of the plan have already become legislation, including fifty billion dollars from the February 2009 stimulus package that focused on green energy projects.[2] The Environmental Protection Agency (EPA) was given seven billion dollars to help the economy become green.[3] Obama's green New Deal had a list of impressive technologies it would develop, including:

Ocean Wave Power

As of August 2004 this technology became a reality when the first tidal energy prototype came on line supplying 500 homes with electricity in the U.K. The prototype was called the Pelamis machine. It was 120 meters long, 3.5 meters wide, weighed 20 tons and could produce 750 kw of energy. Since then, technological progress in tidal technologies has progressed rapidly. New machines are being developed that take up to 50 times less ocean floor space than the original machines and are significantly more efficient and cheaper. In the next 3 years, 30 new wave energy projects are expected to come on line.[4]

According to the United States Department of Energy, as much as 2 terawatts of electricity could be provided by ocean waves alone. The British Wind Energy Association estimates wave power potential to be anywhere between 8,000 and 80,000 terawatt-hours annually. [5] Currently, global electricity consumption is roughly 16,000 terawatt-hours annually.

Nuclear Energy

This is not a new energy source. The first energy producing nuclear reactor was built in 1957. Since then, 2601 nuclear reactors have been built across the world. Because nuclear energy emits almost no carbon dioxide (CO_2) it is likely to be an energy source that the US and other nations increasingly rely on in the future. Currently, nuclear energy provides about 11% of the world's energy needs. As nations become increasingly concerned about global warming and willing to take risks, the number of nuclear reactors is likely to increase. New technologies in fast breeder reactors and different fuels might make nuclear energy a virtually unlimited cheap energy source.

Fusion Power

Capturing the heart of the sun, that is what fusion power promises to do. The sun produces energy by fusing two light atomic nuclei together to form a heavier nucleus. Billions of dollars have been spent to reproduce this phenomenon. It is still in the realm of science fiction, but should it become commercially viable, it would provide an unlimited amount of cheap and clean energy; enough energy to power innumerable cars, televisions, amusement parks, hospitals, and factories.

High Voltage Direct Current

This technology is slightly less science fiction inspired and more realistic and promising. It deals not with energy production, but with transmission. One of the problems with renewable energy sources such as wind and solar, is that the location of the energy source is often far from cities or factories where the energy is used. The Sahara desert in North Africa has enough potential solar energy to supply all of Europe, just as the Gobi Desert can supply all the energy needs of China. The oceans are also rich with wind energy, but are quite a distance from land based power grids. For every 100 km away from the coast, wind speeds increase by about 1 meter per second. The planet is loaded with renewable energy, but the problem is one of proximity. Europe is not close to the Sahara, nor is the Gobi Desert to Beijing. The problem is the transporting of energy.

Essentially all transmission lines are alternating current (AC). They are heavy and inefficient. A large amount of energy is lost during transmission. High voltage direct current lines are a new technology. They are lighter and more efficient. There is practically no limit on how far they can efficiently carry energy. London and Beijing could be connected to far away deserts for their energy needs. Cost is still an issue, but as use increases and technology improves it should become more affordable. A high voltage direct current line seventeen hundred miles long has already been laid in the Congo. In June 2009 construction began on a 130 km direct current transmission line to connect an ocean wind farm located 130 km off the coast of Germany.[6] Laying these transmission lines will make renewable energy more affordable.[7]

In addition to alternative energy sources, Obama's plan calls for increased production and use of energy efficient products. The list of products described as green is lengthy: light bulbs, fridges, cars, planes, ships, houses, buildings and many more. The new Boeing Dreamliner uses twenty percent less fuel than other jets. LED lights use ten times less energy than conventional bulbs and can last a lifetime. An Energy Star labelled fridge will use twenty-six percent less energy than a conventional fridge. The plan is to build factories in the United States that will produce these products, increasing employment and saving the environment.

Wind, nuclear, wave, and green products are some of the technologies in Obama's green New Deal. They are promising, but do face obstacles. Green products have to compete with their often cheaper and more established cousins. Coal, gas, and petroleum, non-renewable and polluting sources of energy, are still the principal power sources and are cheaper than renewable energy.

Renewable energy is catching up though. In the early eighties, wind power cost about 30 cents per kilowatt-hour. Today, according to the British Wind Energy Association, the cost is between 5 and 6 cents. This is only marginally more expensive than coal.[8] The main cost of wind energy is the set up cost. After wind farms are built, the cost of generating energy is almost free. Wind energy is gaining acceptance. More energy from wind power came online in Europe in 2008 than from any other energy source.[8] According to a study done by the European Environment Agency (EEA), energy from offshore turbines alone could competitively provide between 6 and 7 times more energy than all of Europe's anticipated energy demands.[10]

Governments have set daunting pollution reduction goals, both internally and by means of international agreements. Renewable energy sources and more efficient products are the tools governments are using to meet these goals. Like Roosevelt's New Deal, Obama's green New Deal intends to put people back to work manufacturing and selling eco friendly products and constructing a green energy network.

What will the effects be? Will the 'Green New Deal' rescue the economy and the environment?

The underlying assumption in the theory of green growth is that if we create new products that save energy and pollute less, we can grow the economy while reducing our ecological footprint. This win-win situation makes politicians, the business community and some environmentalists happy.

I recently had the opportunity to address this question at a presentation at a local university. I started by asking the audience a question: "which one of these is more ecologically friendly, a gas guzzling SUV or a bicycle?"

The crowd of 4th year environmental science students looked confused and bewildered. "Ok," I said, "everybody who thinks it's the SUV put up your hands". Only one student did not put up his hand. I looked at him. He replied, "I don't know why, but I know this is a trick question."

Unfortunately, this is not a trick question. The answer is not as obvious as we would expect. The answer is that it depends. An SUV would probably cost its owner around $400 a month in insurance, petrol, taxes, maintenance etc. If the owner switches from an SUV to a bicycle, it will save him/her around $400 per month. The operating costs of a bicycle are fairly negligible.

Let's assume that the operating cost of the bicycle is $20 per month. This represents a saving of $380 per month.

Scenario 1

If that $380 were spent, the owner of the bicycle would be increasing his/her ecological footprint again. A European vacation, a new computer or a bigger home all represent minerals being mined, pollution being emitted through manufacturing, energy being used and an ecological impact on disposal.

Scenario 2

The money is not spent; it's literally torn up and thrown away. The ecological footprint decreases, but so does the economy. If enough people switch to bicycles and throw away the money they save, the economy will shrink along with employment opportunities. People take a lot of pride and meaning from the work they do. High unemployment rates have a history of making for politically volatile and even revolutionary times.

President Obama's plan, as well as the United Nations goal of green growth, is a promise of industrial growth and a reduction of our ecological footprint. Only one of these goals will succeed and if it is industrial growth at the expense of ecological sustainability, then growth will be short lived.

Notes:

1. Obama, Barack. Fairfax, Virginia: Address at George Mason University on the 21st Century Economy. January 8, 2009 . Retrieved from: John T. Woolley and Gerhard Peters, The American Presidency Project [online]. Santa Barbara, CA. Available from World Wide Web: http://www.presidency.ucsb.edu/ws/?pid=85361.

2. Kirchhoff, Sue. February 17, 2009. USA Today. *How will the $787 billion stimulus package affect you?* Retrieved from: http://www.usatoday.com/money/economy/2009-02-12-stimulus-package-effects_N.htm.

3. EPA. February 17, 2009. *EPA Information Related to the American Recovery and Reinvestment Act of 2009 (Recovery Act).* Retrieved from: The Environmental Protection Agency website, www.epa.gov/recovery/.

4. Pham, Lisa. October 20, 2009. New York Times. *Waves Start to Make Ripples in Renewable Energy World.*

5. Thorpe, T W. November 30, 1999. *An Overview of Wave Energy Technologies: Status, Performance and Costs.* ETSU, B 154, Harwell, Didcot. Retrieved from: www.wave-energy.net/.../An%20Overview%20of%20Wave%20Energy.pdf.

6. Monbiot, George. 2008. Doubleday of Canada. *Heat: How to Stop the Planet Burning.* ISBN-10: 0385662211. Page 104.

7. Sustainable Development Commission. November 2005. *Wind Power in the UK.* Retrieved from: www.sd-commission.org.uk/wind.

8. Communication From the Commission to the European Parliament, the council, The European Economic and Social Committee and the committee of the regions. November 13, 2008. *Offshore Wind Energy: Action needed to deliver on the Energy Policy Objectives for 2020 and beyond Brussels.* Retrieved from: http://www.europeanenergyforum.eu/archives/european-union/eu-general-topic-file/eu-energy-sources-primary-secondary/eu-renewable-sector/offshore-wind-energy-action-needed-to-deliver-on-the-energy-policy-objectives-for-2020-and-beyond.

9. European Wind Energy Association. (EWEA) Press Release. September 16, 2009.

Chapter 11
Green Energy

New technological innovations in green energy are sparking hopes that a renewable and sustainable industrial economy is possible. Hope that an ecological cataclysm can be avoided and hope that we do not need to make unwanted lifestyle changes. Throughout the centuries, human innovation has conjured solutions to countless environmental and social limitations. Are the current ecological problems that we face no different from the challenges of the past?

Is this just one more scenario where science will come to the rescue?

For the most part, 'green' technology is mostly defined as a technology that makes a product or industry more efficient. The logic is that the more efficient something is, the less of it we need. Efficiency sounds positive and even sexy. The logic seems intuitive and trustworthy. If an energy source is more efficient then surely we will be using less of it. Unfortunately, in most instances this is not the case. Historical evidence shows an inverse and counter intuitive relationship between efficiency and use.

Before the invention of the steam engine, the primary fuel (besides food for people and pack animals) was wood. Wood was used for heating and cooking. Besides the occasional water wheel, this was pretty much it for the majority of human existence or roughly 100,000 years.[1]

During the Industrial Revolution, a new technology made its appearance: steam power. Steam powered trains, factories, and ships began to dot the landscape and usher in the age of fossil fuels. Coal replaced wood as the primary fuel source.

What makes coal such a miraculous improvement over wood is that it is substantially more energy efficient. A pound of coal can produce 12,000 BTU of energy.[2] It requires twice as much wood to produce that amount of energy. If a steam engine ran on wood, one trip across the US would equal 240 seventy-foot high oak trees. If we factor in that the steam engine would need to be about 3 times the size and at least require double the amount of energy, then the journey would need 480 seventy-foot oak trees. An entire forest lost for a single trip.

Petrol is similarly twice as energy efficient as coal. A pound of petroleum yields about 20,000 BTU. It also emits less toxic chemicals into the atmosphere, such as sulfur and mercury.[3]

The lesson of history is that if we define 'green' energy as energy that is more efficient and cleaner, then all technological energy innovations over the last 200 years have been 'green'. Coal was more efficient and had less of an ecological impact than chopping down forests and using wood for energy. Petroleum was more efficient than coal and emitted fewer toxins. Nuclear is more efficient and cleaner than petrol.

How can this be?

The more efficient something is, the less resources and labour is required. In the example of the steam engine it would take 480 seventy-foot high oaks to be burned to make the trip across the US. It would also mean that more labour would be required to chop down the trees and to build locomotives that are twice the size. The ecological cost of losing a forest for each journey would also mean no wood for cooking or home building. To put it simply, the inefficiency of wood as a fuel source made it unfeasible for the demands of the age of steam. More efficient coal allowed us to expand our cities, grow our industry and thus increase our ecological footprint. The same applies for petrol. Transatlantic flights probably would never have been possible under steam power. The weight to energy ratio of coal is just too high.

Petroleum, however, offered the solution. The increased efficiency it offered helped create a massive aviation industry of approximately 450,000 active airplanes. In 2006 more than 2.2 billion people flew. This contributed to three percent of the world's greenhouse gas emissions.[4] Even though petrol is cleaner and more efficient than coal, an industry of steam powered Boeing's would have never taken off.

The mechanics:

Even though we often refer to the efficiency of fuel, cars, and engines, what we are really discussing is the efficiency of labour. The more efficient a fuel source is the less labour is required in obtaining, transporting or using it. A ship running on coal needs to be almost twice the size and requires significantly more labour to build and fuel. A more efficient engine uses less fuel, and consequently, less labour is required to obtain that fuel. A more aerodynamically efficient airplane uses less fuel and potentially can be larger. Consequently, more people can be transported for less labour in the construction of the plane and less labour in obtaining the fuel for the plane.

Notes:

1. Strachan, T. and Read, Andrew P. 2003. Garland Science: New York, NY. *Human Molecular Genetics 3, Volume 3.* ISBN: 0-8153-4182-2. Page 385.

2. ReVelle, Charles and ReVelle, Penelope. 1992. Jones and Bartlett Publishers, Inc: Boston, MA. *The Global Environment: Securing a Sustainable Future.* ISBN: 0-86720-321-8.

3. Hill, Marquita Kaya. 2004. Cambridge University Press: New York, NY. *Understanding Environmental Pollution: a Primer.* ISBN: 0-521-82024. Page 353.

4. Abramowitz, Janet N., Brown, Lester Russell, Renner, Michael, Halweil, Brian, Starke, Linda: Worldwatch Institute. 1999. W.W. Norton and Company. *Vital Signs 1999: The Environmental Trends That Are Shaping Our Future.* ISBN: 0393318931. Page 86.

Chapter 12
What Is Efficiency?

What makes the debate on efficiency so confusing is that there is no clear single definition for efficiency. In some parts of this book we've discussed the productivity of labour, and in other parts we have analyzed the impacts of energy efficiency. When referring to efficient accounting procedures, medical procedures, wind turbines and automation robots, the term efficiency takes on many different meanings and requires different values of measurement. This creates the impression that they are not all linked, but they are.

Even though there appears to be many different forms of efficiency, they all have one thing in common: us. We are the ones who strive for efficiency, in the tools we create, in the design of our cities, in the mechanics of robots, in the utilization of minerals and land. When we discuss efficiency what we are really concerned with is how they impact our lives. This part of the relation is impossible to measure in kilojoules per second or Model T Fords built per hour. It is impossible to measure because it is up to us to decide what we will do with that efficiency. The efficiency of all the machines we have built, software designs and every other kind of efficiency we have sought translate into us becoming increasingly efficient.

From an ecological perspective, if our objective is growth then that efficiency translates into us being more efficient at decreasing the carrying capacity of the planet. The form that efficiency comes in is irrelevant. Our objective of growth is what increases our ecological footprint. Everything that makes us more efficient at achieving that goal is equally detrimental to the ecology.

An efficient accounting procedure, a hospital intake form or even cameras[1] can be just as deadly to the planet as a more efficient automation robot or jet plane.

They all put the identical mandate on the economy: Grow or there will be rising unemployment. The more efficient we become, regardless of where that efficiency comes from still means we have to grow the economy: more products, more waste and more consumerism.

The motive of growth is also not simply a matter of greed. Our history as a species has left a legacy revealing that the nations with the biggest economies and most sophisticated technologies are also the ones with the most powerful armies and ability to enforce their will on less powerful nations. The motive of growth is further discussed in chapter 25.

Notes:

1. Back in the early 90s the first consumer digital cameras were introduced. The advantage of these new more efficient cameras was that you no longer had to send your exposed film to be developed: a costly and labour intensive process. Today photo development lab technicians have become mostly a thing of the past. More efficient cameras meant fewer jobs, but provided more consumers bought cameras and other consumer items, new employment opportunities were created elsewhere in the economy. In 2007 37 million digital cameras were sold in the USA.

Chapter 13
Greenest Planet in the Solar System
Part 1

The following is an example that demonstrates how the relationship between efficiency and the economy can create for an unexpected and unintuitive relationship with the ecology.

In a galaxy far, far away, in a solar system similar to ours, there are two almost identical planets: planet Crystal and planet Stinky Goop.

On planet Crystal, energy is exclusively derived from crystal radiation. It's highly efficient and, except for the occasional radiation leak, it is non-toxic. Because it is efficient it only takes the labour of 10 percent of the population to provide enough energy for the other 90 percent. Because it is relatively non-toxic, only one percent of the population are employed in cleanup and healing people with radiation contamination.

The people on planet Stinky Goop get their energy exclusively from a black sludge that is mined from the earth.

It's not as efficient as crystal energy and it requires a lot of labour to mine enough of the sludge to keep the economy functioning. Approximately 40 percent of the population is required to produce enough energy. Because goop is highly toxic, another 20 percent of the population are employed as doctors and nurses healing sick people and cleaning up spills.

So, which planet do you think is going to win the much coveted greenest planet of the solar system award?

Initially it seems obvious the trophy goes to the Crystal people. Before we announce the winner, let's add to the equation the one thing that regularly derails the best "Green" intentions; the economy.

There are two broad categories of labour:

- Those that provide energy.

- Those that use energy to manufacture products, use these products and build infrastructure such as highways and buildings.

On planet Crystal, 11 percent of the population is employed directly and indirectly in obtaining energy. Consequently 89 percent is employed in using that energy to build buildings, highways, ships etc.

On planet Stinky Goop, 60 percent of the population is employed directly or indirectly in obtaining energy for the economy. Only 40 percent are left building highways, ships,

computers, Nintendos etc...

The efficiency of crystal energy gives both the ability and the need for planet Crystal to have more growth. The ability comes in the form of abundant and easy to produce energy. The social requirement of employment dictates the necessity. Planet Crystal is more likely to have more highways, cities, gadgets, gizmos, planes, ships, buildings, mining, harvesting, and of course more pollution.

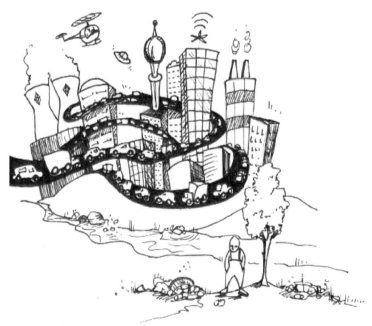

Just as with the spinning jenny and Fords production lines the efficiency of the energy source puts the same type of mandate on the economy: either the economy grows or there will be increasing unemployment. Industrial growth solves the problems placed on the economy but it increases the demands we put on the ecology. The bigger the economy grows and the more resources we use and the more pollution we create the bigger our ecological footprint becomes.

If we think of ecological sustainability without regard to the economy, then we might erroneously think that we can reduce our ecological footprint by becoming more efficient. Once we factor in the economy, the relationship is reversed. The more efficient an energy source, the greater our ecological footprint becomes.

In Part 2 of the Greenest Planet in the Solar System, we will make the example a little more realistic. First, we need to define what pollution is.

If we think of pollution simply in terms of the amount generated from the energy source, then crystal energy is green. If we think of pollution as the result of humans redesigning the planet to suit the needs of just one species on the planet then Stinky Goop is the greener energy source.

Chapter 14
What Is Pollution?

Initially, pollution was waste disposed of into rivers and lakes that made us sick and killed the fish we depended on. It then became toxins in the air from mines and smokestacks that again made us ill and decreased the yield of agriculture and livestock farming. The more our influence on the planet grew, the more we learned that our very existence depends on a healthy ecosystem. Our existence depends on a delicate balance of species of which we are but one. Everything we do that alters that balance is pollution; the cities we build, the roads that crisscross the planet, the mines that produce raw materials, everything.

A definition that is limited to toxic spills and chemical waste ignores the full extent of the problems and challenges that we face.

Chapter 15
Greenest Planet in the Solar System
Part 2

With our new definition of pollution, let's revisit the example of the greenest planet in the solar system. This time the planets are virtually identical except that one has abundant oil and the other has an abundant and easy to generate wave energy.

On planet Wave the energy technology is still in its infancy. As such, it is more expensive. In this example, planet Wave is operating at a 2004 Earth level wave technology. They use big Pelamis machines that weigh 20 tons and only produce 750 Kw energy. On planet Oil, the wells are naturally pressurized and produce light sweet crude. Light sweet crude is the highest quality; it requires very little refining. Since it is easy to access, abundant and requires very little refining it is very cheap: $10 a barrel.

So which planet do you think is going to win the much coveted Greenest planet in the solar system competition? Let's compare three scenarios:

Scenario 1: We ignore the economy and assume that each planet requires the same amount of energy. It's an unrealistic scenario but a popular one for modeling. In this scenario, the planet that builds the least amount of infrastructure to support its energy needs is the one that wins the prize. On planet Oil the process is as simple as drilling a hole in the ground and barrelling the oil as it bubbles to the surface.

On planet Wave, the process is a lot more complicated. First, a complex electrical grid system of thousands of miles of transmitters and cables needs to be laid. Once that is done, millions of tons of iron need to be mined, processed and transformed into the wave to energy converters. If energy consumption is anything like on planet Earth, they will need 16 terawatts (1.585×1013 W) of energy. Since a single Pelamis machine can only produce 750 kw, 21.3 million Pelamis machines, made from 400 million tons of steel, need to be built. From an ecological accounting perspective, the steel, the concrete and all the industrial infrastructure needed to build and run the Pelamis machines need to be taken into account.

The net result; planet Oil wins the competition hands down. Energy that simply bubbles up from the ground by itself is simpler, cheaper and is a whole lot less ecologically damaging.

Of course the above example is unrealistic. It's simply a way to contrast the efficiency of oil versus the inefficiency of wave to energy converters.

Scenario 2: Now let us add a little more reality into the equation by factoring the confusing dynamics of the economy.

Wave energy is less efficient than energy derived from oil because it takes more labour to produce. More people are required to build and maintain the wave farms, mine steel, sit in offices and design the wave farms etc. Compare this to a few oilmen pouring oil into a barrel. The difference is substantial.

On planet Oil, energy is easier and cheaper to obtain. Fewer people are employed in the energy sector. This means more people are available for other sectors of the economy, such as mining, aviation, space travel, automobile manufacture and more. The net result is a bigger economy on planet Oil and a greater demand for energy.

Efficiency, whether in production of cars, clothes or even energy, has the same effect on the economy. The more efficient energy is, the fewer people are employed in obtaining it. Unless the economy grows and people manufacture, use, and waste more there will be rising unemployment.

It is not simply an issue of greed. Increased efficiency insists on either growth or less work being available. The efficiency of oil energy compared to wave energy is what enables and demands a bigger economy. The bigger the economy, the more energy used and the more consumerism on planet Oil results in planet Oil losing its title of 'greenest' planet in the solar system, despite having a more efficient and environmental friendly fuel source.

Sustainability is more about what we do with that energy than where it comes from. It is about how we use or misuse energy to change the functioning of the ecosystem to support only one species.

The above example is of course hypothetical. The competition is not over yet. It is time to add a little more reality into the model.

Scenario 3: This model includes some of the more conventionally defined forms of pollution: toxic spills and carbon emissions. We will also assume that there have been technological innovations on planet Wave and the cost of wave converters has come down.

When it comes to ecological sustainability, things are often not as clear as we would like. It's often speculative, hypothetical and confusing. There is so much we do not understand about the functioning of the ecosystem.

Let's assume that on planet Oil the Oilerians are somewhat lazy and do not bother refining much of their oil. As such, when used it is polluting. The fuel has a high content of lead, sulfur and other toxins (like our shipping oil). These toxins make the citizens of planet Oil ill. The pollution on planet Oil reduces the ability of the Oilerians to grow food and be productive. Economic growth consequently slows.

The carbon emissions on planet Oil are also starting to affect the climate. Global warming, after many years of politicians denying it, is turning out to be a reality. Crops are drying up, freak storms and floods are destroying cities. As their ecosystem worsens, the economy of planet Oil starts to collapse.

The opposite is happening on planet Wave. Planet Wave does not have these problems. Wave energy does not have the same type of immediate visible pollution. The citizens continue to use the energy to grow the economy, unrestricted by health and other immediately visible repercussions. As the technology evolves it also becomes cheaper and more affordable. The new found efficiency enables them to mine, build and consume even more. Their cities double and then triple in size, the number of highways crossing the planet becomes uncountable, ships and planes keep getting bigger and bigger. Because wave energy is cleaner, there is less of a feedback mechanism telling the citizens on planet Wave to stop. The damage becomes more severe and irreparable. Much of what we regard as environmental pollution is really checks with which the ecosystem restricts human industrial expansion.

Technology allows us to remove some of the immediate effects, but it does not remove the real ecological problem. That problem is the idea of unlimited and unrestricted industrial growth. The example is hypothetical, but in my opinion, the planet that can learn those lessons the soonest will be the one that is better off. The more damage we do by modifying the ecosystem to our will, the more severe will be the repercussions.

Ecological sustainability is not a clear cut issue. We are dealing with a complex relationship between the ecosystem and the economy. Two topics that, even independently, we know very little about. When studied together, the dynamics are unintuitive. It is not as simple as what energy source or product is more efficient. The best example that highlights this complex interdependency is not planet Oil versus planet Wave, but rather our own history.

Chapter 16
The Challenges of Being Green

The line between an ecological disaster and ecological miracle can be blurry, scary and depressing. The previous example was hypothetical, but our own history, on which it is based, is real.

Ever since cavemen and women started to use fire for cooking and heating their poorly ventilated caves, air pollution has been an issue of increasing concern.

In 1870, long before cars and power plants, the mining company Rio Tinto was expanding its copper production in Spain. Ore was smelted on the spot, roasted over charcoal in open air piles, drenching the vicinity in sulphuric acid rain. A British commercial agent acknowledged, "Throats and eyes are painfully affected... Under these conditions vegetable life is impossible and animal life is rendered difficult." [1]

The most polluted city in the seventeenth century was London. A writer of the time wrote "a cloud of sea-coal, as if there be a resemblance of hell upon earth, it is in this volcano in a foggy day: this pestilent smoak, which corrodes the very yron, and spoils all the movables, leaving soot on all things that it lights: and so fatally seizing on the lungs of the inhabitants, that cough and consumption spare no man. [2] By

1825, London had surpassed Beijing as the world's largest city, home to 6.6 million people and almost as many coal burning smoke stacks and chimneys. The foulness of the London fog became legendary. The toxins in the air routinely laid people to rest before their time. Approximately 3000 people died as a result of aggravated lung conditions, presumably caused by air toxins in the winter of 1879 and 1880. [3]

In the early twentieth century the most polluted region in Europe was the Ruhr, the industrial heartland of Germany. By 1910 it produced 110 million tons of high sulphur coal, employed 400,000 miners and sustained the giant steel and iron works of Krupp and Thyssen. The sky was permanently a dull grey. People were regularly sick. Even crops growing in surrounding areas took twice as long to grow. [4]

Japan's determined efforts to industrialize and catch up to European levels of growth resulted in it having comparable air pollution levels. A fisherman whose livelihood was destroyed by the Yawata steelworks reflected, "With the development of the Japanese nation, and the development of this region, it is us the fisherman who have become the victims."

Cities in the United States were similarly plagued by air pollution. The bigger the industry, the greater the pollution. Air pollution was a way of life in St-Louis, Chicago, Pittsburgh, New York, and many other cities. [5]

Journalist Waldo Frank wrote of Chicago in 1919, "Here is sooty sky hanging forever lower... The sky is a stain: the air is streaked with running of grease and smoke. Blanketing the prairie this fall of filth, like black snow - a storm that does not stop..."

Even though there was a will in countries and cities to do something about pollution, there was reluctance on the part of businesses to bear the costs. The argument was that clean air would be expensive and bad for the bottom line. If factories were forced to  bear the costs they would surely lose their national competitiveness and be forced to relocate, or worse, shut down. Fearful politicians were reluctant to risk their cities' economy and refused to enact effective clean air legislation.

One of the first cities to reverse this trend was the American city of St-Louis. Engineers, citizens and even some members of the business community got together to enact an effective smoke prevention law in 1940. Despite the cost of installing cleaner burning smoke stacks, the economy of St-Louis did not deteriorate. The air became cleaner and citizens were happier and more productive. As it turned out, cleaner air was good for business.

This profitable example inspired many other cities. Pittsburgh was the first to follow suit in 1941. This was accomplished despite objections from coal interests. In addition to better built smoke stacks, they converted to cleaner 'greener' fuels such as natural gas, oil and anthracite.[6] London and New York followed this example and an international trend ensued. Cities across the world converted to cleaner burning fuels and introduced stricter air quality laws.

Japan enacted the strictest air quality legislation by 1961. This did not hinder it from also becoming one of the fastest growing economies in the world. Clean air was good for the citizens of Japan, the farmers, the fishermen and for business. By 1990, Glaswegians who ordinarily inhaled two pounds of soot each year had reduced sulfur and dioxide pollution by 70 to 95 percent.

In many ways, the success of cities in cleaning up smog pollution is an environmental success story. It is also an important environmental failure. When cities switched over to cleaner burning fuels that were more efficient and polluted less it allowed industry to expand. Previously, growth was hampered by pollution which decreased productivity and made the industry in cities less desirable.

Cleaner, more efficient fuels and technology enabled cities to grow, expand into newer production technologies, and accommodate more cars and highways. The more cities grew, the more energy they consumed, the more pollution they created and carbon dioxide they emitted.

Previously, the problem was toxins and foul smelling air. Today, the problem is 23,431,741 tons of carbon dioxide being released into the atmosphere and causing climate change.[7] We swapped an ecological problem for an ecological nightmare.

In many ways, the pollution we create is the check and balance that keep us from increasing the damage we ultimately do to the ecosystem. Economists refer to this as negative feedback. Each time 'green' technology enables us to overcome negative feedback we abuse the opportunity by expanding production and consumption.

We see a similar pattern in paper and pulp mills. They use a wide range of highly toxic chemicals such as cyanide, arsenic, chlorine, mercury and lead. If not treated correctly these chemicals can have an immediate and dramatic impact on the local environment.[8]

Due to the easily visible effects of paper and pulp mill pollution, neighbouring residents and local officials have been quick to demand strict legislation enforcing environmental cleanup. Even banks and other financiers are insisting on more environmentally friendly production techniques.[9] Business has realized that cleaner production techniques will result in less resistance from local communities.

The paradox is that if our goal is to reduce our impact on the environment, it isn't working. In 1970, the planet's paper production was approximately 126 million tons. 298 million tons of paper was produced in 1997. About 40 percent of the world's industrial wood harvest is used to make paper.[10] Even when only new growth forests are harvested, it still represents a substantial negative impact on the natural ecosystem. The majority of the 298 million tons of paper will be disposed of in toxic landfills, breaking the cycle of organic matter re-nourishing the earth. Paper accounts for approximately half of all the space in landfills in the US.[11] Newspapers consume 41,000 trees daily.[12] Per capita consumption of paper has increased from nearly 18 to 50 kg between 1950 and 1997.[13]

Again, an ecological victory became another one of our biggest failures. The problem we have is that our objective is 'growth'. When it comes to the environment, if we are cleaning up because of a business model that makes economic sense, the net result is even more damage.

Notes:

1. McNeill, J.R. 2000. WW Norton. *Something New Under The Sun.* ISBN-10: 0393049175. Page 85.

2. Ibid, page 57.

3. Ibid, page 66.

4. Ibid, page 86.

5. Ibid, page 67.

6. Ibid, page 69.

7. WRI, 2003. Carbon Emissions from Energy Use and Cement Manufacturing, 1850 to 2000.Available on-line through the Climate Analysis Indicators Tool (CAIT) at http://cait.wri.org. Washington, DC: World Resources Institute.

8. Pandey, Ashok. 2004. Haworth Press: Binghampton, NY. Concise Encyclopedia of Bioresource Technology. ISBN: 1-56022-980-2. Page 145.

9. Clay, Jason W. 2004. Island Press: Washington, DC. *World Agriculture and the Environment: A Commodity-By-Commodity Guide to Impacts and Practices.* ISBN: 1-55963-367-0. Page 325.

10. Brown, Lester, Russell, Brian, Halweil and Renner, Michael. 1999. W. W. Norton & Company: New York, NY. *Vital Signs 1999: The Environmental Trends That Are Shaping Our Future.* Pages 78–79.

11. Gore, Albert. 2000. Houghton Mifflin Books: USA. *Earth in the Balance: Ecology and the Human Spirit.* Page 151.

12. Hamelman, Steven L. 2004. University of Georgia Press: USA. *But Is It Garbage: On Rock and Trash.* Page 27.

13. Brown, Lester, Russell, Brian, Halweil and Renner, Michael. 1999. W. W. Norton & Company: New York, NY. *Vital Signs 1999: The Environmental Trends That Are Shaping Our Future.* Page 78.

Chapter 17
What About Recycling?

Increasing levels of efficiency is the cause of our ecological problems and not the solution. This peculiar and confounding mandate extends to even the most honourable of green intentions: recycling.

We want to believe that we can reduce our ecological footprint by recycling, and we can. But just as with every other 'green' initiative, if it is adopted for the wrong motives then it will have an undesirable ecological consequence: industrial growth and not a healthier ecosystem.

A good clue that a green initiative is being misused is the business model. If a technology has a business model that makes sense for corporations, it is probably not good for the ecology.

A recycled can not only uses less energy, but also requires less mining, less metal processing and of course less labour. A recycled can cuts out a lot of jobs.[1] Lost jobs need to be created elsewhere in the economy. To create these jobs, we inevitably seek to do what we always have done: grow the industrial economy with more production, construction, mining and consumerism.

The problems of recycling become compounded when we delve deeper into some of the other business motives behind recycling. I live in the beautiful city of Vancouver. Just as with most cities, developers and politicians have great plans for the expansion of the city. Their goal is to increase the

Greater Vancouver District to be almost fifty percent bigger within 10 years.[2] To accomplish this, 5 billion dollars is being spent on new bridges, bigger highways, a new shipping port and more roads. Thousands of acres of farmland will be tarred, developed and converted into an expanding concrete jungle.

There is however a stumbling block: garbage. Vancouver and its surrounding neighbourhoods produce a lot of it. They produce so much that they have run out of places to put it. The local area dumps are all full beyond capacity. Currently, garbage is trucked 250 miles to the Cache Creek landfill. This dump is now near capacity. The city has literally run out of places to put its waste. Without a garbage solution, the dreams of developers along with the size of the city, are restricted.

Unfortunately for the ecology the province and local cities have found solutions to the problem of garbage restricting their aspirations for growth. Technology, conveniently labelled as green, is coming to the rescue. Firstly, they are encouraging more recycling. Secondly, they plan on installing six solid waste incinerators; big furnaces that will convert garbage into energy. The process also releases harmful toxins into the atmosphere. [3]

I am not saying that recycling is bad. I am saying that if the motive is growth, then the ecological implications will reflect that.

Notes:

1. All money paid goes to somebody for his or her labour effort. There are no extra terrestrials or earth spirits or any other creatures except us humans that charge and receive money (hopefully). Every penny that is paid is eventually received by a human for their labour effort.

As such, the labour cost is equivalent to the product cost of an item. If a recycling project has a business model that proves that it can save money, it means that less money is being paid to somebody for some type of labour effort.

If labour is being remunerated at the same rate (labour/time) for a new product vs a recycled product, then the a reduction in the cost of the recycled product represents a reduction of labour hours involved in production. The argument in this case hinges on the assumption that remuneration rates for a recycled product are equivalent to those for a new product. This will not always be the case. As such, this form of accounting for labour hours only serves as an approximation. Because of the scope of the economy and the amount of transactions that occur for any given production task, it is probably impossible to get a better estimate of labour hours.

2. Retrieved from: The City of Port Coquitlam website: www.portcoquitlam.ca.

3. Lewis, Brian. The Province. August 27, 2009. So many new challenges for Sumas 2 vanquisher: FVRD chair responsible for booming area twice size of P.E.I. Retrieved from: http://www.theprovince.com.

Chapter 18
What About Electric Cars?

These days the news is awash with stories of the demise of General Motors. The world's largest automaker was forced into bankruptcy in May 2009. According to GM, they had US$172.81 billion in debt and US$82.29 billion in assets.[1]

What if they had made more fuel efficient eco-friendly hybrids or electric cars? President Obama himself has criticized the management of GM for misreading the markets and making cars Americans no longer wanted. The demise of GM has cost American taxpayers 50 billion dollars.[2] Could GM and the bailout money have been saved if only GM had gone green?

There is a saying, "What is good for GM is good for America."[3] Once you factor in the iron mined for cars, the highways built for them, the plastic, the batteries and the coffee cup holders, the number of people indirectly employed by GM becomes a sizable percentage of the population. A car requires 6000 to 13,000 parts, most of which come from independent contractors. GM directly employs 266,000 people around the world. However, according to David Cole head of the Center for Automotive Research (CAR), the number of people indirectly employed is much higher. Approximately three million jobs would be lost if American automakers shut down.[4]

Could manufacturing smaller more fuel efficient cars have saved GM and been good for the economy? For the sake of the argument, let's assume that the US Congress is correct and that Americans truly do want more efficient green cars.

One example of an eco or allegedly "green" car is the Reva electric car. It weighs 565 kg (1,250 lb) and has a range of 120 km (75 mi) on a single charge and has a top speed of 80 km/h (50 mph). A regular combustion engine has more than 700 moving parts. An electric engine has only one; the brushes of the electric generator that can be easily replaced every 11,000 miles or so and cost $20 a brush. The engine of an electric car is virtually maintenance free.

The average car weighs about 2500 kg (4000 lb), about five times the weight of the Reva, which means that the Reva will only consume one fifth the amount of steel, rubber, paint, etc. Fewer resources go into making the REVA and it is also a lot smaller. Furthermore, they take up a lot less space on highways, streets and parking lots.

If Americans switched to 'green' cars, it might mean an initial boom in sales, but it would also mean that over the long term fewer people would be employed manufacturing and repairing cars, supplying parts or building roads.

The greater efficiency of the 'green' car translates into fewer jobs. If this were the end of the story, it would be a great victory for the ecology. A victory for the ecology but not one readily accepted by humanity and the economy. To rescue the economy and create more jobs the impetus again becomes increased levels of production, construction and of course consumerism. Jobs lost are jobs that need to be replaced. The repetitive tale of efficiency and growth iterates itself one more time: the more efficient we become, the bigger our ecological footprint becomes. Green intentions are simply not enough to break out of this ecological downward spiral.

This is not cause to give up hope. Once the problem is understood, solutions become simple and relatively easy to implement.

Notes:

1. PBS Online News Hour. June 1 2009. *GM Files for Bankruptcy Protection; Judge OKs Chrysler Asset Sale.* Retrieved from: http://www.pbs.org.

2. Associated Press. June 1, 2009. Bankruptcy first step in 'new GM'.

3. Half a century ago, in 1953, General Motors Chairman Charlie Wilson declared, "What was good for our country was good for General Motors, and vice versa." Retrieved from: Quinn, James. March 3, 2009. The Cutting Edge. *As General Motors Goes, So Goes the Nation.*

4. Doran, James. The Observer, The Guardian UK. November 16, 2008. *Crash of US carmakers risks three million jobs.* Retrieved from: http://www.guardian.co.uk.

The figure of 3 million jobs includes jobs lost if all the American auto makers shut down. It includes both direct and indirect employment opportunities.

5. Unless the hours of work are reduced or some form of efficiency shifting is implemented. This is discussed later on in this book.

Chapter 19
A Green Conclusion

What will be the outcome of the world's drive towards a 'green' industrial future?

Will the economy grow and more jobs be created? This will depend on the types of technologies adopted. Currently, the objective is to increase the levels of efficiency: more efficient planes, cars, buildings. The long term implication is a commitment to growth in order to keep people in the economy employed.

A future of green efficiency is not a new idea. New more efficient technologies and correspondingly increased levels of consumption are the history of the Industrial Revolution. It's what got us into this mess in the first place.

PART 4
Solutions

Faced with climate change and a myriad of other ecological problems, our fate seems uncertain, but it need not be. Real and easy to implement solutions do exist. The major obstacles we face are not ecological constraints, but rather insufficient understanding of the interconnection between the ecology and economy.

Solutions are simple and possible.

.

Chapter 20
Efficiency Shifting

With increasingly dire news about the state of the ecology it is clear that we have a problem. Now all we need is a solution. Do we put our faith in new green technologies that will make us more efficient or do we simply consume less?

Both solutions seem to have undesirable repercussions. Increasing levels of efficiency seem to rebound into perpetual growth and consumption. Consumers spending less seem to trigger warning bells of imminent recessions and higher unemployment rates.

I recently attended a forum on ecological sustainability. Towards the end, the consensus seemed to be that the only solution was to get rid of our cars, buying less and growing our own food. Unfortunately, a little old lady in the front piped up "wouldn't we destroy the economy and cause massive unemployment if we did that?" The mood in the room dropped a notch or two because whether we liked it or not the little old lady was right.

The options before us at this pivotal junction in time seem to be either a world with massive unemployment (if we consume less)[1] or one with the extinction of countless species including our own (green growth).

A third and more viable option is needed; one that recognizes the relationship between efficiency, consumerism and our ecological footprint. Such a potential solution is efficiency shifting.

Our error has been to view the economy as a single entity in which every component needs to become increasingly efficient. This is not the case. There are many sectors that could benefit from increasing levels of inefficiency. If the efficiency gains in one sector were counter balanced with inefficiency in another sector, the growth impetus of the economy would effectively be muted.

An example of an efficiency gain could be a factory that uses increasingly sophisticated automation technology or a car that is lighter, smaller and uses less fuel to run or to produce. The net effect of these efficiency gains would be that fewer people would be employed in the production of these cars unless consumption increases.

An example of an inefficiency gain could be legislation requiring an increasing percentage of agricultural output to be organic. Organic farming is more labour intensive than conventional farming.

Jobs lost as a result of automation or more efficient cars are replaced in a different sector of the economy. Efficiency gains counterbalanced with inefficiency. The benefit would be that employment would remain constant despite the economy not growing.[2] We would also have the benefit of more ecologically friendly farming as well as cars and industry that pollute less. A double benefit to the ecology, stable employment rates and an internally dynamic economy are all possible at the same time.

The first step in adopting a process of efficiency shifting would be to identify the sectors of the economy that we could all benefit from becoming increasingly efficient. This is the easy step. The second step would be to identify the sectors of the economy where we would all benefit from adopting some level of inefficiency. There are many such sectors in the economy such as farming, health care, social work and education.

The concept of efficiency shifting is not complicated and does not need hundreds of pages of graphs, charts and indecipherable equations to explain. It is really simple. The biggest challenge this idea faces is the almost religious dogmatic belief in 'efficiency' by not just taxpayers, economists, politicians and the business community, but by environmentalists as well.

Notes:

1. If the work week is reduced many of the negative consequences of rising unemployment can be mitigated. This is topic dealt with in part 4 of the book.

2. The reason why the overall economy does not grow is that the efficiency impetus is being counter balanced with inefficiency and not increased consumption of products.

The competitive incentive to innovate still exists as different manufacturers compete to gain market share. As such, there will still be an incentive for competing manufacturers to innovate with increasingly efficient product technologies.

Chapter 21
Organic Farming

When most of us think of organic farming, we think of two dollar peaches and apples with tiny pockmarks that cost a fortune. Organic food is expensive, even the relatively wealthy seem to be a little troubled by the price. Although we can't seem to afford organic produce these days, there was a time when we could.

Organic farming is expensive because it is labour intensive. Large monocrops of thousands of hectares of beans or cotton are not possible for the organic farmer. They attract a feeding frenzy of little critters. Imagine you are a little bug that loves tomatoes and you come across a farm with thousands of hectares of them: pure buggy heaven. Miles and miles of tomatoes are not a diverse ecosystem providing habitat to a natural balance of predators. Bugs get a stress free, eat and breed lifestyle. If it were not for billions of tons of nasty toxic chemicals called pesticides, these large farms would not produce much food, at least not for humans.

There is, however, a huge ecological cost to non-organic farming. Once sprayed on crops the industrial toxic brew made up of DDT, organochlorine and methoprene not only kills the hungry little pests, but also the birds that feed on the insects, while polluting rivers and contaminating the entire food chain. The species that are most in decline are those that are most sensitive to these toxins. Many of these are part of the amphibian family. Thirty-two percent of amphibian species are currently threatened, forty-three percent are declining in population. The Global Amphibian Assessment lists 427 species as "critically endangered." [1]

The more the earth's natural habitat gets converted to farm use and the more pesticides get dumped on that land, the more inhospitable this planet becomes to millions of species.

There are possibly over a hundred million different species of insects, animals, and fish. Only 1.4 million have been identified. Even fewer have been studied.[2] When it comes to ecology we really know nothing. Most of the species that have gone extinct are species whose existence we were unaware of. Gone before we even knew what essential role they played in keeping this planet functioning.

Species extinction could be a bigger threat to humanity than global warming. Unlike global warming where we can predict increases in temperature, we know too little about the ecosystem to even know how much trouble we are in.

In addition to polluting and destroying the habitat of so many, industrial farming also strains the availability of one of our most precious resources: water. Currently 61 percent of all water is used by farming. A very visible effect of the overuse is the decline of the water levels of the Colorado River, which now carries less water than at any time in recorded history. Some years it even no longer reaches the sea. Underground water aquifers are also being drained faster than they can be replenished. The Ogallala Aquifer, which is bigger than any of the lakes in North America, is losing one meter from its water table every year. By some estimates it is already half depleted.

Overuse of underground water supplies in the Central valley has resulted in a loss of over 40 percent of the combined storage capacity of all human made reservoirs in the region.[3] The future of the United States is a thirsty one if it continues with its current agricultural farming practices. The problems created by industrial farming practices are certainly no secret. Even the Central Intelligence Agency has listed water scarcity as a factor contributing to future global instability.

Industrial farming presents the world with a bleak, violent, and thirsty future. For many the solution is new more efficient farming technologies, drought resistant crops and technological wonders. In other words, more of the technologies and ideas that got us into this mess in the first place.

An alternative approach is the reverse. Add inefficiency back into the production of food. Increasing amounts of efficiency caused our problems, adding inefficiency back can solve them. Inefficiency in farming has the biggest potential to solve climate change, species extinction rates, environmental degradation, poverty and even hunger.

It's hard to believe, particularly for a world enamoured with the gospel of efficiency.

Efficiency, whether in the manufacturing of textiles and cars, or in farming practices, has the same basic effect. It means that we can produce so much more with less labour. The consequence is that we then either need to consume more or face the prospect of rising unemployment and the instability that it brings. That's what efficiency does.

Now let's look at how adding inefficiency back into farming can reverse the damage being done. A good example of an inefficient form of farming in terms of labour input is organic farming.

The organic farmer needs to carefully blend a variety of plants that create a natural sustainable ecosystem that can remain in balance without the aid of toxic chemicals. Large monocrops are not possible, so the organic farmer can't rely on as many sophisticated machines. From sowing the seeds to harvesting the crops the entire process requires more labour. It is also more labour intensive to sell an organic crop. Instead of delivering all produce to one purchaser, multiple crops need to be sold and delivered to different locations.

The solution that organic farming offers is not just a product that has less of an ecological impact on the ecosystem but more importantly offers opportunities for employment. Thus it offers opportunity for efficiency gains in other sectors of the economy, which are more detrimental to the ecosystem, to be counterbalanced with inefficiency gains in agriculture. In other words, efficiency shifting.

How might efficiency shifting work?

The more efficient industry becomes, the fewer people are needed to manufacture products. Rather than trying to grow the economy and get people to continually consume and waste, it is possible to enact ethical farming practice legislations that increases the percentage of organic farming. There are countless ways that this can be done, from restrictions on the size of farms (as was done in the 1930s) to taxing the use of pesticides.

An example:

A new, more efficient car production plant is developed. The consequence is that less labour is needed to produce cars. Our response as a civilization has been to find new ways to increase consumption or waste. The more efficient industry becomes, the more we produce, the more we consume and waste, the bigger the economy grows and the greater our ecological footprint becomes. A way to break this cycle is to make something else in the economy less efficient. In this example, let's assume we increasingly transition to organic farming.

The result is that the efficiency gains from the production of more efficient goods do not result in industrial growth. More efficient automobile production means that fewer people are employed in this sector. But if done in conjunction with increasing levels of organic farming, the growth impetus of efficiency is cancelled out by inefficiency in farming.

Automobile manufacturers still have the incentive to innovate and get an increasing percentage of the market, but overall consumption levels do not increase.

This has a lot of relevance for our current drive to new 'green' technologies, such as more efficient cars, airplanes and buildings. Without efficiency shifting, these technologies will result in fewer jobs for a fixed level of product output. The traditional solution of policy makers is to grow the economy to increase employment. If we allow this to happen, all the benefits of these new green technologies are lost.

One of the biggest criticisms and arguments against organic farming practices is that it is expensive and will result in poverty and starvation. This is not correct. Despite almost a century of cheap and abundant food, poverty and starvation has been increasing. The relationship between poverty and expensive food is the reverse in many cases. If done correctly, more expensive food can help reduce poverty and hunger. This is the topic of the next chapter.

Notes:

1. The IUCN Species Survival Commission. 2004. *2004 Global Species Assessment.* Edited by: Jonathan E.M. Baillie, Craig Hilton-Taylor and Simon N. Stuart. Authors: Jonathan E.M. Baillie, Leon A. Bennun, Thomas M. Brooks, Stuart H.M. Butchart, Janice S. Chanson, Zoe Cokeliss, Craig Hilton-Taylor, Michael Hoffmann, Georgina M. Mace, Sue A. Mainka, Caroline M. Pollock, Ana S.L. Rodrigues, Alison J. Stattersfield and Simon N. Stuart. Available at: http://data.iucn.org/dbtw-wpd/edocs/RL-2004-001.pdf.

2. Tokeshi, M. 1998. Wiley-Blackwell. *Species Coexistence: Ecological and Evolutionary Perspectives.* ISBN-10: 0865427445. Page 139.

3. Barlow, Maude and Clarke, Tony. 2003. Earthscan Ltd. *Blue Gold: The Battle Against Corporate Theft of the World's Water.* ISBN-10: 1844070247. Page 16.

Chapter 22
Why Cheap Food Creates Poverty

In 1900 approximately one third of the population were employed in agricutlure. Today it is about 2.7 percent. [1]

What changed this relationship to the earth and farming was mechanization, nitrogen fertilizers, pesticides and automation. The family farms of the past became the mega food factories of today, swallowing up thousands of hectares of land and resources. The most significant technological innovation in this transition was the mass production of the tractor: another one of Henry Ford's inventions. In 1910, there were 25,000 tractors in the US. In 1917, Henry Ford introduced the Fordson, which was cheap and mass produced. In the short span of three years the number of tractors grew to 246,000. [2] A single farmer could now till, harvest, and sow hundreds of acres without an army of labourers. As it was so much easier and cheaper to produce food, the price of produce fell. Millions of farmers and farm labourers lost their jobs and migrated to the cities.

That is what technology does. With less labour we can produce so much more. Unless we consume more, we end up in a recession, or worse, a depression. The tractor and other mechanization technologies gave us the mass production of food. Mass production of food required mass consumption. Wasteful mass consumption did not exist at that time and rural farming collapsed.

To solve the problem, President Roosevelt (in his New Deal) came up with a strategy to limit the output and size of farms as well as protect the welfare of small farmers. The Agricultural Adjustment Administration (AAA) was created in May 1933. There was also the Resettlement Administration (RA), the Farm Security Administration (FSA) and the Rural Electrification Administration (REA).

Roosevelt's New Deal, and similar legislation that followed, limited food output and through increased scarcity, forced the price of food up to pre-1913 levels. Laws that limited output and more expensive food were extremely unpopular. However, they worked.

With fair food prices and labour intensive practices, more people were able to farm and live a rural lifestyle. With less rural poverty, fewer people migrated to unemployment lines and soup kitchens in the city.

The attempt to keep farms relatively small, and thus limiting their output, came to an end in the 1970s. In 1971, under Nixon, Earl Lutz became the secretary of agriculture. The legislation protecting small farms were thrown out the window. The objective now became to produce, produce more and keep it cheap. "This year 1973 we are going to see the most massive increase in the production of farm products ever in the history of this country," stated Earl Lutz. [3]

Output doubled, then tripled, and the prices dropped. Large factory farms were able to take advantage of the newest technologies in mechanization, pesticides and later, genetics. Small family run farms were no longer competitive and went out of business. Employment in agriculture, once the largest employer fell to 2.7 percent. Quaint rural farms were transformed into large industrial food producing factories.

Small towns emptied and people sought the promise of the city.

Today, the average American will spend less than 10 percent of their income on food. This includes restaurants, take out and everything else. This is about half of what our great grandparents used to spend. In most years from 1929 to 1952 it was above 20 percent. [4] The greatest age-old dream of a cornucopia of cheap plentiful food became a reality.

This reminds me of another age-old saying. Be careful of what you wish for, you might just get it. The dream of unlimited and cheap food has become our single biggest ecological nightmare, as well as a source of poverty around the world. Just as cheap food increased hunger and poverty during the Great Depression it is creating poverty and starvation today.

Today a billion people around the world live in slums. Food has been getting cheaper, but hunger and poverty have increased. According to the Food and Agriculture Organization Director General Jacques Diouf, an estimated 963 million people, or 14 percent of the world's population, are unable to afford to eat enough calories to lead a normal life.[5]

In 2008, a massive study called the *International Assessment of Agricultural Knowledge, Science and Technology for Development* concluded that the immense production increases brought about by science and technology in the past 30 years have failed to improve food access for many of the world's poor.[6]

How did this happen?

With the agricultural produce of North America doubling and then tripling, the challenge became what to do with it. Output tripled, but the mouths to feed in the USA did not. The population in the United States between 1970 and 1980 only grew by five percent. Even with the most gluttonous of diets, they could not have eaten it all. Part of the solution was to export the majority of it.

In 1970, the US export market was only seven billion dollars. By 1980, it had grown to 44 billion dollars. An increase in net volume of 170 percent. The US share of the world market for wheat and flour grew to 48 percent. For grain it was even higher at 60 percent. [7]

Mechanization, automation, new fertilizers, and government subsidies to agro-business gave the US farming industry a competitive advantage over farmers in third world countries who still relied on more traditional and communal farming practices. Cheap corn, chicken, beef, grain and more flooded economies foolish enough to open their markets to cheap American produce. The consequence was that traditional farming communities went out of business. Millions of farmers, and those that depended on them were forced to move to cities in search of work.

Massive rural unemployment gave rise to sweatshops: large labour houses where there were no annoying unions to protect workers from exploitation. Farmers and their families now became the manufacturers of cheap shoes, televisions, radios and bouncy toys. Sounds like a good deal for Americans: cheap food in exchange for a plethora of cheap stuff. Unfortunately it has had a few unforeseen repercussions in the United States as well.

Cheap food has had an ill effect on the diets of the American population. One of the solutions for dealing with the mountains of cheap corn and cheap grain was to feed them to animals. It takes approximately seven pounds of grain to produce one pound of beef.[8] The cheaper agricultural produce became the more it was used to feed livestock. Cheap animal feed and large livestock factory farms pushed the price of meat down. Large inhumane factories of tens of thousands of animals became increasingly common across the country. The cheaper meat became, the bigger a component of our diets it represented. U.S. beef and pork consumption has tripled since 1970.[9] A diet of fresh healthy vegetables and grains gave way to one of hamburgers, steaks and ribs.

According to a large federal study, people who eat the highest levels of red meat and processed meats such as hot dogs, bacon and cold cuts are about 20 percent more likely to die of cancer compared with people who eat less than five ounces per week. With heart disease, researchers found heavy red meat consumption increased the risk of death for men by 27 percent and for women by about 50 percent. [10]

The ecological impact of livestock farming is devastating. Growing food to feed animals means that more of the earth's natural space is getting burned, ploughed and filled with toxic chemicals than necessary. According to the British group Vegfam, a ten acre farm can support 60 people growing soybeans, 24 people growing wheat, 10 people growing corn or only two producing cattle. Meat based diets are very land and resource intensive. The smaller the percentage of meat is in our diets, the less land is needed to be dedicated to its farming. According to a 2006 UN report, domestic farm animals contribute to 18 percent of climate altering greenhouse gas emissions.[11]

So here is a quick summary of the problems caused by cheap food:

- It's cheap, so we feed it to animals and then eat the animals. This means that we are using between 10 to 15 times more of the earth's space for ecologically damaging industrial style farms.

- Cheap food is being dumped into developing nations' markets, destroying their communities and creating poverty.

- It's unhealthy.

- It only provides 2.7 percent of the population with jobs.

How organic farming solves these problems:

- Better income distribution. Organic farming is labour intensive. Depending on the level of organic farming practiced, as much as 60 percent of the population could be employed in this sector. With unemployment rising, this could be an essential sector where important meaningful work needs to be done.

- Organic food is way more expensive. Feeding it to animals and then eating organic animals is costly. Consequently less of the earths' surface will be dedicated to growing food to feed to animals.

- The more expensive food becomes, the less likely it is to be dumped on third world economies. This gives third world economies a greater financial incentive to become agriculturally sustainable. The more rural communities are healed, the less pressure there is forcing people into sweatshops.

- The primary health benefit of an organic diet is that it has less meat. Free-range animals fed on organic produce would be prohibitively expensive. The more expensive it becomes the less meat people will consume. It is not healthy to eat meat three times a day.

The idea that more expensive food is better for people is a concept that's hard to believe. The proof is in the history and consequences of cheap food. More expensive food means jobs not only for North Americans, but people across the world. It enables better income distribution so that not just the wealthy can afford to dine on meat while a billion people starve.

One of the most common criticisms is that farm labour is menial work. It's surprising that this idea would exist. Why is it that being locked up in a cubical staring at a computer and shuffling papers is more meaningful than growing healthy food?

Notes:

1. John O'Sullivan, Edward F. Keuchel. American Economic History: From abundance to constraint. Page 96

2. Jeremy Rifkin. The End of Work. Page 111

3. King Corn(2007). Directed by Aaron Woolf. With Earl L. Butz, Ian Cheney, Curt Ellis.

4. USDA, Economic Research Service, Food CPI and Expenditures report, Table 7

5. United Nations, Food and Agriculture organization press release, 26 January 2009, Madrid

6. Beverly D. McIntyre Hans R. Herren Judi Wakhungu Robert T. Watson .Agriculture at a cross roads 2008, International assessment of Agricultural Knowledge, Science and technology for Development

7. Willard Wesley Cochran. The development of American agriculture. Page 151, 200

8. Harvey Blatt. America's Food: What You Don't Know About What You Eat. Page 134

9. Donald W. Lotter. Earthscore: Your Personal Environmental Audit and Guide. Page 18

10. Reducing Meat Consumption Has Multiple Benefits for the World's Health Barry M. Popkin, Arch Intern Med. 2009;169(6):543-545.

11. The Food and Agriculture Organisation of the United Nations. Livestock's Long Shadow - Environmental Issues and Options. November 2006

Chapter 23
More Efficiency Shifting

Depending on the level of organic farming, it could solve many of our ecological and economic problems. However, it is not a solution for everyone. I, for one, don't wish to return to the land and be woken by roosters. Fortunately, there are many other sectors that could benefit from becoming less efficient.

The idea of accounting for every second on a production line has a long history that began with Henry Ford's goals of making cheap mass produced cars. The Ford Motor Company made efficiency into a science. Process engineers armed with stopwatches carefully accounted for every second of every task. Assembling a magneto took 13 minutes and 10 seconds. A transmission cover took 9 minutes and 20 seconds. Building a complete model T chassis took 1 hour and 33 minutes. [1]

Once the times were recorded, engineers would study the results and find new ways of improving efficiency. Every second meant lower costs and quicker turnover. Time saved was money earned.

It did not take too long before bureaucrats became enthralled with Henry Ford's stop motion studies and decided to try the same techniques with social services, such as health care and education. The cost accounting techniques of the industrial economy were moved over to the caring economy. The logic was that every second saved meant taxpayers and patients saved money. In industrial style hospitals, patients become job sheets with carefully tabulated amounts of services required. Everything was accounted for, from the number of pills to be dispensed to the expected number of bedpan changes. If a patient took longer than expected to recover, or required more services, the efficiency rating of that ward or hospital unit would go down. If it dropped below a certain point, the stopwatch-armed process engineers would return to find out what was going wrong. Efficiency became something that could be accounted for, it was used as a basis for allocating rewards as well as a basis for justifying dismissals and pay cuts.

What was lost in transferring stop motion studies to the caring economy was caring. Too difficult to account for and even more difficult to put a price tag on. If a nurse or doctor spent time listening to the troubles of a patient or giving any additional attention, efficiency ratings would go down. Caring becomes penalized in a world where everything is based on efficiency. The more hospitals, schools and other social service facilities that adopted the accounting techniques of industry, the more they became like factories. The object was to fix, repair, read, and show instead of educate or heal. The end result is a disaster. What was good for cars and washing machines was not good for people.

The ratio of students to teachers is on the rise again in the US. Local governments, in a bid to balance their budgets, are increasing classroom size. This is happening despite all the research that conclusively shows that students perform better in smaller classes. Classrooms with 20 or fewer students have been shown to dramatically increase learning as well as graduation rates.[2] The more students a teacher can teach creates statistics that show the schooling system is more efficient. More efficient means taxpayers or parents save money. The benefit of a better educated society gets lost in statistics that are only concerned with saving money. An educated society is a society that is better equipped to deal with whatever challenges the future brings.

The problem with the focus on efficiency in the education system goes much deeper than this. What evaluation does occur is done based on national or state exams. Teachers and schools are rewarded based on the test results of their students. The problem is that what gets studied is how to pass the exam and not the subject itself. The thinking and passion gets lost in favour of thousands of students studying what the answers to questions should be. Education becomes boring and to a large degree useless.

Education is vital to the survival of a prospering society. Every generation will be presented with new challenges and problems to solve. Their success depends on the lessons they have learned and their abilities to solve problems.

As for the health care sector, becoming efficient was not enough. Over the years, public hospitals have been shut down in favour of private hospitals. Private institutions have an increased incentive to be efficient. The more efficient they become, the more profit they can make. Between 1996 and 2002, the number of public hospitals declined by 26 percent. The consequence is an efficient system that can perform many expensive procedures and tests, but has no time to stop to listen or care. The consequence is that Americans spend 2.3 trillion dollars on medical bills. This is more than any other nation. Even though the system is very efficient at performing expensive and profitable procedures, it is not effective in caring for people. According to the World Health Organization, health care in the United States ranks only 37th in the world.

When caring is lost in health care, the ethics follow suit. The most difficult health problems to account for, using cost accounting and stop motion studies, is psychiatric services. There are often no physical wounds to heal or bones to mend. The healing process often requires time and caring. With few physical tangibles this is a sector that has had the most cut backs.[3] Unable to get funding or sufficient remuneration, mental health hospitals (both public and private) have been closing down. With no place to go, the mentally ill often end up on the street. Of the estimated 744,000 people who are homeless in the United States on any given night, 40 to 45 percent of them have a serious mental illness. As the street is no place to recover, many eventually end up in prisons. According to the Federal Bureau of Justice 2006 statistics, there is an estimated 1.25 million prison inmates who suffered from mental health problems. A five fold increase since 1998.[4] The current solution to deal with the mentally ill is to leave them on the street or lock them up.

Adapting ideologies of efficiency to education and healing have in many ways crippled these sectors. The net result is that the most expensive medical system often delivers third world results. An education system with lots of graduating students that won't be able to manage critical problems that the nation will be increasingly faced with.

The contradiction is that there is no shortage of labour. The more technology makes industry efficient the fewer people are required to manufacture goods. Infinitely trying to consume more to put people back to work is no solution. We need to find meaningful and important work. Education and health are vastly more important to the well being of a society than the manufacturing and disposal of things we do not need. A focus on efficiency has crippled these sectors. It is time to free them by making them inefficient. We need more people employed, with less focus on efficiency and greater opportunity for caring.

Our problem is one of a single-sided perspective: that efficiency is the elixir that all sectors of the economy need to benefit from. It is the belief that we should save taxpayer's money without recognizing all the essential benefits that a healthy, educated and competent population has to offer. Education and health care are part of the public sector. The public sector is there for the benefit of all citizens. Every educated healthy person is a benefit to everyone who is part of society.

Notes:

1. Beaudreau, Bernard C. 2004. Authors Choice Press: Lincoln, NE. *Mass Production, the Stock Market Crash, and the Great Depression: The Macroeconomics of Electrification.* ISBN-10: 0595323340. Page 8.

In the case of vehicles, the term chassis means the frame plus the "running gear" such as the engine, transmission, driveshaft, differential, and suspension.

3. Appelbaum, M.D, Paul S. American Psychiatric Association. October 2002 © 2002 American Psychiatric Association. *Starving in the Midst of Plenty: The Mental Health Care Crisis in America.* Retrieved from:
http://psychservices.psychiatryonline.org/cgi/content/full/53/10/1247
.

4. Written by BJS statisticians Doris J. James and Lauren E. Glaze. Press release: 6 September, 2006. Bureau of Justice Statistics. Based on report NCJ-213600.

Chapter 24
Reducing the Work Week

Many academics of the fifties and sixties thought the future would be one of increasing leisure time. Even President Kennedy believed it was a solution to deal with the increasing number of layoffs as a result of automation. During a speech he made in 1963 he talked about a better future for

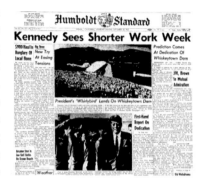

America, "This country is changing. We had a 58 hour week, a 48 hour week, a 40 hour week. As machines take more of the jobs of man, we will see the work week reduced."

As we are all well aware, the future has turned out very differently. Instead of increasing hours of leisure we found ourselves on a treadmill trying to infinitely match increased production with increased consumption. Working longer and harder to manufacture more products.

Fortunately for the ecology of the planet, many European nations did choose to take their productivity gains in the form of reduced hours. France, Germany, Norway, Denmark and Sweden all reduced their work week.[1] The average American will work about 460 hours more a year than the average Dutch or Norwegian. That's about two and a half months less work.[2] Consumption level in these countries is a lot lower than in North America. According to a paper from the Center for Economic and Policy Research, if Europeans increased their work week to match that of Americans, they would consume 30 percent more energy. Pollution and carbon emissions would increase. [3]

An argument that is often used against a reduced work week is that it will reduce the gross domestic product of a nation. This is hopefully true, but it is also likely to result in a more egalitarian income distribution.

The following chart plots the income gap between various nations.[4]

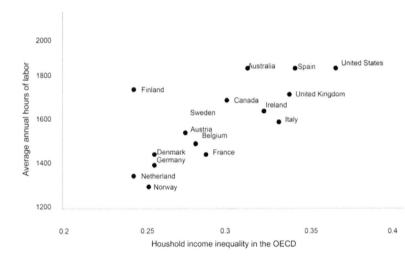

The country with the smallest income gap between rich and poor (egalitarian) is the Netherlands. It is also the country with the second shortest annual hours of work. The country with the biggest income gap is the United States. It is also the country with the longest hours of work.

It is not a perfect correlation, Finland being one major exception. Finland is the second most egalitarian nation but has a fairly average number of hours of work.

In general the more leisure time a nation has, the more egalitarian it is. The graph is not conclusive proof of a causal nature. But a fair hypothesis is that having leisure time gives citizens an opportunity to get involved in community, find out what their politicians are up to, educate themselves on issues and connect with people with similar interests. Having time is essential in creating an empowered citizenry. Empowered citizens are in a better position to demand a more egalitarian income distribution and greater benefits for the average person.

In the United States, real wages have not increased since the seventies despite increasing productivity. The efficiency gains from industry have mostly gone to the wealthy. From 1947 to 1979, the top sliver of wage earners made about 20 times that of the bottom 90 percent. By 2006, that ratio had catapulted to 77 times more. Data on income concentration going back to 1913 shows that the top one percent of wage earners now hold 23 percent of total income, the highest inequality level in any year on record, except for 1928. Overall, 26.4 percent of workers earned poverty-level wages in 2007.[5]

The citizens of the United States are working longer, harder and more productively than ever before, but the benefits are increasingly slipping away.

Even though politicians and government are always accountable, the question is to whom. In the case of the

United States, in 2008 corporations spent 3.3 billion dollars on lobbyists and donations to candidates that best represented their interests.[6]

Simply being the people who created the majority of this wealth is not enough. Citizens need to become a force to which politicians and government are accountable. This means more than simply voting for one of two very similar candidates every four years. What makes a nation strong and just is a government that serves the interest of the majority of its citizens. What makes a government serve the interest of its people are people who insist that they do so.

A reduced work week helps people achieve this empowerment in many ways. Primarily, it distributes the workload so that more people are employed. Unemployed people, who are potentially facing homelessness, are more concerned with finding a job, or their next meal, than politics or economics. Democracy is stronger when there are less people in this state of dire need. Secondly, it gives people the opportunity to become involved. Overworked citizens who spend long hours commuting or furiously trying to meet a deadline do not have the time, inclination or social connectivity to be a political force.

Since I left my job programming automation software, I have been promoting the idea of reducing the work week. Initially, people treated the idea as if it were complete insanity. More and more it's being taken seriously. To help get media attention to the concept, I started a political party called the Work Less Party in 2004. We ran in the federal and civic elections in Canada. The purpose was not to get candidates elected, but rather to get the idea of a reduced work week discussed at candidate debates. The party did surprisingly well for an organization whose purpose was not to get elected. In the 2008 Vancouver civic elections we received over 40,000 votes. One of the surprising questions we were often asked was, "Surely if we work less won't we have more time to damage the environment?" For many who asked the question, the answer was completely unacceptable.

A reduced work week helps reduce our ecological footprint by shrinking the economy; work less, produce less and consume less. The size of our Gross Domestic Product is the best indicator of the size of our ecological footprint. The damage we do to the ecosystem is mostly about the resources we use in the production of products and the pollution created in manufacturing and disposal. For our ecological footprint to decrease, we need to produce and waste less. For many, the idea of shrinking the economy is completely unacceptable, as they fear it will result in a decrease in living standards. This is not the case.

First, it gives people the time for things like education, health, family and more. Secondly it helps prevent the wealth of a nation being concentrated in the hands of a few.

With better income distribution and less wasteful consumption we can all afford to work less. The average worker today, in just 11 hours of labour, can produce the same amount of goods as the average worker working for 40 hours in the 1950s.[7] If we are willing to accept the same level of product consumption as someone working in the 1950s for 40 hours, we could all be on a two day work week. Oddly enough, in many ways people in the fifties in the US had a higher standard of living than today. Education was more affordable and houses were comparatively cheaper. It is true that there were fewer cars, but public transport was vastly superior. The only real major difference was that less was wasted. Today we work longer, harder and produce more, but 99 percent of everything we produce ends up in a landfill six months after it was purchased.[8]

Work less, produce less, waste less and live more.

Notes:

1. Mishel, Lawrence, Bernstein, Jared and Shierholz, Heidi. 2007. Cornell University Press. Economic Policy Institute. *The State of Working America 2006/2007. International comparisons: How does the United States stack up?* ISBN 0-801489-62-8.

European nations, chose to take their productivity gains in the form of reduced hours — through shorter workweeks, longer vacations, and earlier retirements. This is an explicit policy choice. France, for example, reduced its workweek from 39 to 35 hours in January 2000.

2. Rosnick, David and Weisbrot, Mark. 2006. Center for Economic and Policy Research: Washington, DC. *Are Shorter Work Hours Good for the Environment? A Comparison of U.S. and European Energy Consumption.* Retrieved from: http://www.cepr.net/documents/publications/energy_2006_12.pdf.

3. Rosnick, David and Weisbrot, Mark. 2006. Center for Economic and Policy Research: Washington, DC. *Are Shorter Work Hours Good for the Environment? A Comparison of U.S. and European Energy Consumption.* Retrieved from: http://www.cepr.net/documents/publications/energy_2006_12.pdf.

4.The graph is based on data from: shel, Lawrence, Bernstein, Jared and Shierholz, Heidi. 2007. Cornell University Press. Economic Policy Institute. *The State of Working America 2006/2007. International comparisons: How does the United States stack up?* ISBN 0-801489-62-8.

For annual comparisions of 2003, 2004, 2005 visit:
http://www.efficiencyshifting.com.

5. Mishel, Lawrence, Bernstein, Jared and Shierholz, Heidi. 2007. Cornell University Press. Economic Policy Institute. *The State of Working America 2006/2007. International comparisons: How does the United States stack up?* ISBN 0-801489-62-8.

6. Quarterly lobbying disclosure reports filed with the Secretary of the Senate's Office of Public Records (SOPR) and posted to their website.

7. Rauch, Erik. *Productivity and the Workweek.* Data obtained from from the US Bureau of Labour Statistics, including both manufacturing and services. Retrieved from: http://groups.csail.mit.edu/mac/users/rauch/worktime/.

8. Leonard, Annie. *The Story of Stuff.* Available for viewing at: http://www.storyofstuff.com/.

Chapter 25
Japanese Luddites

Is it possible to simply say no to growth and jump off the treadmill that continuously tries to match increased production efficiency with increased consumption? A million and one chart-wielding economists will tell you no. But economists represent a very small percentage of the population and they get most things wrong.

An example of a nation who did say no to technological innovation was Japan in 1639.

In 1639, Japan began a legislated policy of isolationism called *sakoku* ("closed country"), which marked the beginning of two and a half centuries of isolation from the west. All westerners and their technology were banned and outlawed from Japanese soil. The only exception was a small man-made island named Dejima. Because it was not part of true Japanese soil, a small amount of trading with the Dutch was permitted there. On Dejima, a school was set up. Its purpose was to carefully study the foreigners, their technology and to learn how Japan could defend itself from the foreigners. This was called *Rangaku*, which literally translated to "Dutch Learning".

Japan at the time had a very hierarchical ruling structure, bureaucratically intensive, but stable. Westerners, their technology, their religions and customs were seen as a potentially destabilizing threat to the political and social structure of Japan. Put in the greater context of Western colonialism in Africa, South America and Asia, their decision was probably correct. Trade with western nations did have a tendency to be destabilizing.

For the next 250 years, Japan focused on maintaining its agrarian economy. Being a farmer was regarded as a very honourable position and ranked higher in social class than merchants and businessmen. Industry was shunned. Japanese traditional craftsmanship, from weaving to sword making was protected. Guns, steam technology, the spinning jenny and other potentially competing technologies were not permitted. Recognizing the needs for ecological sustainability laws protecting the forests of Japan were passed. No trees could be cut down without a replacement or, at the very least, a substantial amount of bureaucratic hassle. For the next 250 years the economy of Japan stagnated. It was a period of unprecedented peace.

In 1639 when the foreigners, were evicted from Japan it was far from a voluntary eviction. But they did not have a military advantage over Japan and could do little to resist the eviction. With the armies at similar levels of technological evolution and Japan having a clear strategic advantage, war was not an option. Japan, at that time, could have defended itself.

Thousands of miles away in the British North American colonies events were transpiring that would dramatically change the Japanese way of life. The American colonies followed the European model of industrialization. They embraced technology and adapted to the social changes that it brought. Their economies and military might grew. In 1783 thirteen of these colonies became the United States of America. They had become a world leader in weapons technology, steam and much more. Factories grew and military might strengthened.

In 1853, four United States of America warships ships sailed to Japan under the command of commodore Mathew Perrie. The four ships were the Mississippi, the Plymouth, the Saratoga, and the Susquehanna. It was not a big squadron from any standpoint, but from a technological perspective it  completely dwarfed anything that the Japanese had. Swords and arrows were no match for steam-powered gun ships. Commodore Mathew Perrie's orders were to force Japan to open its borders and begin trading with the United States. The Japanese called the four ships the black ships, because they were partly steam driven. The coal fuelled ships were covered in black soot that filled the air with a dark cloud of smoke. The term black ship eventually became synonymous with all western technology.

Japan succumbed and abandoned its isolationist policy. This is not how the story ends however, but rather how it begins. Japan recognized that in order to protect itself from colonial nations more was needed than simply studying their technology on a remote island. Many Japanese students were sent abroad to western universities. Foreign engineers were commissioned to help build Japanese factories, mines and ore processing facilities. Japan adopted the western industrial growth model. The samurai were replaced with a mechanized army. Swords were replaced with Gatling guns, sailing ships were replaced with a modern navy. By 1855, Japan had its first steam powered warship. By 1867, Japan already had eight western style steam warships under the command of admiral Enomoto Takeaki, who had been a scholar in the Netherlands and was fluent in English and Dutch.

As Japan's industry and armies grew so did its need for fuel and resources. Being an island and given its proximity to the ocean Japan has no significant mineral resources. In order to acquire the resources needed and additional markets, Japan began its own policy of colonization.

In January 1876, Japan employed gunboat diplomacy to pressure Korea to sign the Treaty of Ganghwa, which granted extraterritorial rights to Japanese citizens and opened three Korean ports to Japanese trade. Korea was not enough. In order to continue to expand their industry, Japan needed additional markets and resources. In particular, iron, rubber and oil. To this end, Japan set her sights on East Asia, specifically Manchuria with its many resources. By the beginning of the Second World War, Japan was the dominant colonial power in Asia.

Japan demonstrates how it is possible for an economy to not be based on a growth model. It is also an example of the biggest pitfall of such an economy. A stagnant economy lacks international competitiveness. At the turn of the nineteenth century that competitiveness was in the form of gunboats and military might. Today it is in the form of powerful multinational corporations and trade agreements. Nations with the strongest economies and biggest armies have the persuasive power to sign favourable trade agreements that put weaker nations at a disadvantage.

The problem with this growth model is that it has become outdated. There was a time when nations that adopted the most sophisticated technologies became the most powerful nations, but this is no longer true. The growth model has both social and ecological limitations.

Social limitations:

The more technologically efficient industry becomes, the less labour is needed to produce the same amount of product. The process makes human labour redundant. Our value, our contribution in the cycle, diminishes unless we consume and waste more. If we do not, we face rising unemployment and mass poverty. Just as our grandparents were comparatively thrifty and frugal, our children and grandchildren will need to consume and waste more product than us. The relationship is one of increased per capita consumption to match gains in efficiency.

Research demonstrates that what makes people happy is not owning great amounts of stuff, but rather human bonds, family, friends and meaningful activities.[1] Depression and suicide rates are up. The sale of antidepressants has become a 24 billion dollar industry.[2]

There are likely real limits to how far we can push the disconnect between social well being and the continuous evolution of consumerism.

Ecological limitation:

The fastest growing economy is China, regularly posting double digit growth rates. The growth has come at a cost. Approximately half a billion people do not have access to safe drinking water. Only one percent of the population's 560 million city dwellers breathe air that is considered safe by EU standards.[3] More than 300 million Chinese drink unsafe water tainted by chemicals and other contaminants.[4] The Chinese government's policy to reclaim land from lakes between the 1950's and the 1980's has caused lake areas to shrink by 243 million square meters, or one third of the original area. The coastline is so swamped by red algae tides that large sections of the ocean no longer sustain marine life. Industry and agriculture use nearly all of the flow of the Yellow River, before it reaches the Bohai Sea. A report by the Chinese Academy of Environmental Planning in 2003 estimated that 300,000 people die each year from ambient air pollution.[3] Death rates from cancer rose an astronomical 19 percent between 2005 and 2006.[4] Lung, liver and pancreatic cancers are now the main causes of death. China has also become the world's largest emitter of greenhouse gases contributing to global warming.

In 2031, if the economy continues to expand at the rate of eight percent per year, China's income per person will reach the current US level. Given a roughly equal rate of consumption, the Chinese population would consume the equivalent of two-thirds of the current world's grain harvest and paper consumption would be double the world's current production. Say goodbye to the world's forests. China is also potentially becoming the next environmental disaster. If China were to have three cars for every four people, as in the US, it would have 1.1 billion automobiles. Currently, there are 800 million cars in the world. To provide roads and parking to accommodate such a vast fleet, China would have to pave an area comparable to the land it now plants in rice: 29 million hectares (72 million acres). The immense population would use an estimated 99 million barrels of oil a day; the world currently produces only 84 million barrels a day.[5]

The nation with the biggest economy is the US. Americans constitute five percent of the world's population but consume 24 percent of the world's energy. Fifty percent of the wetlands, 90 percent of the north-western old-growth forests, and 99 percent of the tall-grass prairie have been destroyed in the last 200 years. Everyday an estimated nine square miles of rural land are lost to development. The average American generates 52 tons of garbage by age 75. The average individual daily consumption of water is 159 gallons. The Great Lakes are shrinking. Upstate New York's reservoirs have dropped to record lows and in the west, the Sierra Nevada snow pack is melting faster each year. The government projects that at least 36 states will face water shortages within five years because of a combination of rising temperatures, drought, growth, urban sprawl, waste and excess.[6]

In a world of limited resources and fragile ecosystems, nations that work as hard as possible to use as many resources as fast as possible are only gaining a short term advantage. In the long-term there are three major consequences:

- Irreversible contamination of natural life support systems.

- High dependence on scarce resources that are subject to international competition. Aggressive foreign policies to obtain resources will lead to reprisals. Even the smallest countries have the potential to cripple the largest economies of the world.

- A further weakening of community strength. Neglecting communities creates a weaker society. Real impoverishment is an overworked, tired, and unhealthy population who do not have the personal empowerment necessary to rescue the system.

In the future the economic model of industrialization, with ever more efficient technologies, is more likely to weaken nations than strengthen them. Even though it was a more successful formula to be a colonizing nation instead of a colonized nation, it has limits.

Notes:

1. Richard Layard. Happiness: Lessons From A New Science. ISBN 0-713-99769-9.

2. IMS Health. March 9, 2005. Fairfield, CT. *IMS Reports 2004 Global Pharmaceutical Sales Grew 7 Percent to $550 Billion.* Retrieved from: http://www.imshealth.com

3. Kahn, Jeseph and Yardley, Jim. NY Times Magazine: August 26, 2007. *Choking on Growth: As China Roars, Pollution Reaches Deadly Extremes.* Retrieved from: http://www.nytimes.com/2007/08/26/world/asia/26china.html.

4. Lyn, Tan Ee. September 19, 2009. Vancouver Sun. *'Cancer villages' are the legacy of China's economic expansion: Rivers and lakes are laden with heavy metals and other toxic materials expansion.* Retrieved from: http://www.vancouversun.com/sports/Cancer+villages+legacy+Chin a+economic+expansion/2011723/story.html.

5. Brown, Lester R. January 25, 2006. The Guardian. *A New World Order.* Retrieved from: http://www.guardian.co.uk/society/2006/jan/25/china.guardiansociet ysupplement.

6. Associated Press. October 27, 2007. Msnbc. *Crisis feared as U.S. water supplies dry up.* Retrieved from: http://www.msnbc.msn.com/id/21494919/.

Chapter 26
Conclusion

" They said Ned Ludd was an idiot boy. That all he could do was wreck and destroy, and he turned to his workmates and said: Death to Machines, they tread on our future and they stamp on our dreams " - Robert Calvert, 1985

As the story has it, Ned Ludd was a clumsy awkward fellow who lived in the late eighteenth century. Local kids often teased him because of his clumsiness. On one occasion, after being taunted by local youth, he furiously chased them into a nearby knitting factory. The kids were too quick for him. Darting in between the machines in a fit of rage or clumsiness, he wound up smashing one of the machines. From that day forward, whenever a machine mysteriously got damaged or destroyed, the locals would say, "It must have been that Ned Ludd again."

The Luddite movement, which evolved many years later, took its name after this clumsy folklore hero. The real Ned Ludd probably never lived to see the emergence of the movement bearing his name. A movement of tens of thousands of anti-technology activists who smashed machines, participated in covert military actions and brazenly engaged the British army in battle united under the banner of the fictitious and thus highly elusive General Ludd. Whenever the British army would ask, "Who burnt these factories down?" the townsfolk would timidly reply, "It was General Ludd, sir." The general was everywhere,

Nottingham, London and Manchester! In the army of Luddites everyone and no one was General Ludd.

General Ludd remains elusive to this day. Who knows, maybe it is time for him to return. An option in the struggle against redundancy is to reunite under the banner of the great general and take to smashing machines and shunning technology. It would be a return to a life when our labour was still of value. Craftsmanship and patience would be the operative words in construction. It would mean stepping back in time to unravel the damage that we have done to the ecology and the economy.

Before we reach this complete level of rejection of technology, there are other approaches that could be implemented that are less of a complete culture shock. They also have more potential to be effective than simply canning all human ambitions of technological advancement.

Efficiency shifting gives us an alternative to the return of Japanese isolationist policy or a Luddite revolution. With correct balancing it is possible to invest in technology provided that it is counterbalanced in other sectors of the economy.

In our rushed society the word inefficiency comes with a lot of negative connotations. This need not be the case. Being inefficient, in many cases, simply means taking the time to do something right. Humans do not function like robots and should not be measured using the same definitions of success. As my friend Doris used to say, "We are human beings, not human doings." Our time should and could be about the quality of our lives and not about the quantity of product.

There are many potential forms of efficiency shifting. The one that is the most urgent is most definitely a shift to more sustainable farming practices. This is where the bulk of damage is being done to the ecology.

Other areas for efficiency shifting are better education and health care systems. The benefits to the ecology would not be as pronounced as in the agricultural sector, but it would create opportunities for us humans to enjoy this world we live in.

One of the errors we often make is to think of ecological sustainability as a major sacrifice. The majority of the stuff that is polluting the planet is stuff that we did not really want or need in the first place. Even though this kind of waste has important purpose it lacks meaning. The purpose of waste is to keep employment levels high, but when we work to fill up landfills we lose the opportunity to do and learn meaningful things.

The biggest challenge to the concept of efficiency shifting is that it is certainly not intuitive. The solution that most academics, politicians and environmentalist believe in is increasing levels of efficiency. The solution this book puts forward is increasing levels of inefficiency to counterbalance the growth impetus of increasing levels of efficiency. Unchecked efficiency gains result in either rising unemployment or exponential growth. Efficiency gains without any counterbalance are the cause of our environmental problems and instrumental in our economic problems.

Efficiency shifting is both simple and essential.

Appendix A
Financial Empowerment of Consumers

The architecture of a culture of consumerism would require the financial empowerment and protection of workers / consumers. This would involve government becoming involved in what was then regarded as the affairs of business.

The Great Depression would have been a Rubicon which capitalism would not have crossed unscathed. The laissez-faire view of capitalism popular at the time assumed that the less government interfered in the affairs of business, the better off the nation would be. Herbert Hoover, elected to the presidency just months before the Wall Street crash of 1929, stated, "It is just as important that business keep out of government as that government keep out of business."

It was not just President Hoover and the Republicans who believed in laissez-faire capitalism. At the beginning of the Great Depression, both the Democratic Party, led by Franklin Delano Roosevelt, and the Republican Party, led by Hoover, were pro big business. In 1931, University of Chicago economist Paul Douglas asserted that, "both the Republican and Democratic parties are now primarily business parties, operating consciously or unconsciously through their policies and ideas to protect the interests of the owners of industrial and commercial capital, and they do not represent the interests of...the urban and town wage-workers and farmers."[1]

Capitalism and free markets were popular, but the Great Depression produced a powerful counterbalancing sentiment. Starvation, massive unemployment, mass migration and rampant homelessness were not issues to be meekly accepted among American citizens. Radical ideas of socialism and communism began to be whispered through the masses. By 1933, unemployment had reached 15 million - a quarter of the work force. In the 1933 election, over a million people voted for the Communist party or some radical alternative. It may seem surprising that it was not even more. And it was not only the unemployed whose ideologies were making a turn. Workers increasingly felt insecure in their jobs. As the Depression worsened, they were often asked to accept pay cuts in order to keep their jobs.

The fairly recent blood bath of the Communist Revolution in Russia was still on peoples' minds. While this had been an uprising against a largely totalitarian style of government, it nonetheless added pressure on the US government to end the Depression. Under President Roosevelt, the government was forced to re-examine the fundamentals of laissez-faire capitalism.

The problem was that under laissez-faire capitalism there were few regulations that protected workers rights. Minimum wage and social security were non-existent; workers had very little or no negotiating capacity. Prior to the president's second New Deal, government used to actively support corporations in their fight against unions.

As production efficiency soared through the twenties, so did the profits of the wealthy. One percent of the population controlled 50 percent of the wealth of the nation. Real wages of the working class only increased marginally. Production output was increasing, but citizens' capacity to consume was not. Much of the growth in the twenties was facilitated by citizens going into debt to buy the goods that they could not afford.

American citizens simply could not afford to buy all the goods being produced. For the economy to recover from the Great Depression citizens needed to be financially empowered.

Most of the work that President Roosevelt did through his industrial recovery plan was to try and achieve this financial empowerment. The tools were legislation, work creation projects and the empowerment of unions.

Unions were pivotal to Roosevelt's strategy. They represented a power block that could strengthen the purchasing power of consumers. The workers earning money for their labour were also the consumers buying most of the goods they were producing. If unions could strengthen the bargaining power of workers, then by the same token, they could also strengthen the purchasing power of consumers. The previous ten years of real wage stagnation had to be reversed. Strong supportive American unions could also rally the required political support Roosevelt needed to stay in office.

The president approved the unionization of major industries such as steel and automobile manufacturing. His pro-union stance gained him the support of the Congress of Industrial Organizations, (CIO), though some unions, such as the American Federation of Labour (AFL) remained neutral.

In 1935, Roosevelt created the National Labour Relations Board (NLRB) which had the power to issue cease-and-desist orders to employers the board believed guilty of using unfair labour practices in interstate commerce, which included discrimination against union members in employment and advancement. The board also frowned upon employers who interfered with union organizing. Like many New Deal agencies, the NLRB was staffed mostly by radicals (sometimes communists) attracted to Washington during a time of reform and rapid socio-political change.

Unions thrived. From 1932 to 1940, membership went from 2.1 million to 9 million. The number of union members further increased during World War II when the War Production Board, another creation of the Roosevelt administration, demanded that employers accept unions or face loss of their government contracts. Unions, in turn, promised not to stage strikes or hold up production.

Some employers resisted. Montgomery Ward chairman Sewell Avery said no to unionization. Roosevelt first sent government officials, then U.S. marshals, and finally, the National Guard, to take possession of the company's Chicago headquarters. Avery, who refused to leave his office, was picked up out of his chair by soldiers who deposited him on the sidewalk, an event enthusiastically photographed by the press.[2] Avery's "lesson was not lost on the nation's employers," one labour historian has written.

So intimate had the relationship between organized labour and Roosevelt become by 1944 that the CIO played an important part in FDR's selection of Harry Truman as his running mate. Angry Republicans purported that Roosevelt's campaign managers were under orders to "clear it with Sidney," meaning that any policy demanded the approval of Sidney Hillman, president of the Clothing Workers Union.[3]

Membership in the two largest unions, the AFL and CIO, rose to 15 million by the end of World War Two and the power of organized labour seemed to be a permanent fixture. [4]

Notes:

1. Sean J. Savage. Roosevelt, the party leader, 1932-1945. Page 17

2. John Faber. Great news photos and the stories behind them. Page 86

3. William Safire. Safire's political dictionary. Page 129

4. Robert A. Dentler. Practicing sociology: selected fields. Page 101